The Anunnaki Series

1

The Anunnaki Ulema Book of Enlightenment:
Metaphysical study of the path of wisdom and
esoteric knowledge

Book # 7, from the Series:
The most important aspects and characteristic features of
the Anunnaki and extraterrestrials

Maximillien de Lafayette's books are available in 2 formats:
1-Amazon Kindle edition at www.amazon.com
2-In paperback at www.lulu.com
http://stores.lulu.com/maximilliendelafayette

Date of Publication: September 21, 2010.
Printed in the United States of America. Published by Times Square Press. New York.

Visit the author's bibliography website at:
www.maximilliendelafayettebibliography.com

Acknowledgment and Gratitude

I am deeply grateful to the Anunnaki-Ulema:
Master Li,
Master Mordechai ben Zvi,
Master Sorenztein,
Master Oppenhemier,
Master Kanazawa,
Master Ghandar,
Master Govinda,
Cheik Al Mutawalli,
For without their guidance and contributions, this book would
have remained stacks of papers in my drawer.

The Anunnaki Ulema Book of Enlightenment:
Metaphysical study of the path of wisdom and esoteric knowledge

Book # 7, from the Series:
The most important aspects and characteristic features of the Anunnaki and extraterrestrials

*** *** ***

A publication of
Federation of Ufology & Anunnaki Scholars, Scientists, Historians & Authors

Times Square Press. Elite Associates International
New York
2010

Table of Contents

*** *** ***

10

***   ***   ***

Chapter 3: The Astral Body "Your Double"...71

*** *** ***

How to Talk to Spirits, Ghosts, Entities, Angels and Demons: Techniques & Instructions: The Most Powerful Commands and Spells

This book is unique and extremely useful for many reasons. Mainly, because it provides both the experienced and the beginner with the necessary guidance, ways and techniques to communicate with various kinds and categories of entities. In addition, it instructs the seeker how to comply with rules and pre-requisites to follow during a séance. The author has placed a strong emphasis on: The language of the spirits, ghosts, entities and Arwaah. What should we do when we hear the voices of entities during a séance? The most powerful commands we can use during a séance, and how to order the summoned entities to grant us most needed favors and assistance in urgent matters, as well as general commands pertaining to health conditions, the removal of difficulties in getting a job, the protection of our home from evil spirits, obtaining an immediate financial relief, so on. The reader should pay attention to the instructions pertaining to a direct conversation with summoned entities, and especially to the protocol in communicating with spirits. This is the first book ever published in the West that deals with these topics. The contents and ideas presented in this tome are based upon the teachings and lectures of enlightened masters, who have practiced this etheric art for centuries. Therefore, you should open your mind, and read this book with extreme attention to the instructions provided by the Ulema. Contacting spirits and entities is a serious responsibility. They will respond to you if you follow the spirits' protocol, as explained in the book

The New De Lafayette Mega Encyclopedia of The Anunnaki(6 Volumes)

The world's first, largest, most authoritative and complete encyclopedia on the Anunnaki, their offspring, remnants and extraterrestrial civilization on Earth, from the beginning of time to the present day.

Thousands of words, entries, definitions and subjects in English, Akkadian, Sumerian, Assyrian, Ugaritic, Phoenician and languages of the ancient world. Abundance of illustrations and photos of slabs, seals, inscriptions, statues, tablets, monuments, archeological sites, and maps.

Translation of Sumerian-Akkadian tablets. The Encyclopedia covers, studies and explains all the facets and aspects of the Anunnaki, and the civilizations they created on Earth.

In-depth articles on so many levels: linguistic, etymological, epistemological, philosophical, historical, religious, mystical.

A masterpiece!

Anunnaki Genetic Creation of the Human Races, Demons and Spirits. 3rd Edition

1. The Anunnaki gods and goddesses who created the first humans, and the genetic creation of the human race.
2. The Igigi created the first quasi human/robots.
3. The Akkadian text on the creation of Man.
4. Anunnaki geneticists who developed DNA sequences, and altered the genes of hybrids.
5. The early human forms.
6. The Earth-made human creatures.
7. The Space-made human creatures.
8. Metabolism and the oceans-made human creatures.
9. Evolution of the extraterrestrials and the human races.
10. Negative entities, reptilians, Djinns, Afrit, evil-birds, and demons which live in the lower sphere/zone (Alternate dimension), and on Earth.
11. Anamidra explains the creation of Man from cosmic clay.
12. Copies of the universe, including copies of ourselves, and Earth.
13. Dual nature of humans, before they were separated genetically.
14. The "Grays": Intraterrestrial non-human.
15. How the Anunnaki created us genetically in their laboratories.

*** *** ***

A Note From the Publishers

A Note From The Publishers

Maximillien de Lafayette wrote more than 70 books on the Anunnaki, including the 6 volume encyclopedia set "De Lafayette Mega Encyclopedia of Anunnaki, Ulema-Anunnaki, Their Offspring, Their Remnants and Extraterrestrial Civilization on Earth." In other words, he wrote more than 30,000 pages on the subject.

To many readers, his work is overwhelming. Consequently, many topics and important subjects were lost in the immensity of information and findings provided in all of his massive published work. It was too much, too large, and too varied. This created some inconvenience and difficulty in finding subjects of interest to many readers.
The world of the Anunnaki is immense, and so too is the work of Mr. de Lafayette.
For example, if you have not purchased all of his books, and/or if you did not classify/categorize a subject you are interested in, it would be impossible to have direct and easy access to the subject or topic you are interested in.
Where would you find an article on an Anunnaki's life on their planet?
The Anunnaki genetic creation of the human race?
How the Anunnaki created religions on Earth?
The habitat of the Grays?
The habitat of the hybrid race?
Chronology of the Anunnaki on Earth?
The return of the Anunnaki in 2022? And so on...

You do admit, it is a hard task to find these subjects without going through the entire body of Mr. de Lafayette's work.

This convinced us that – in the best interest of the readers – we should provide the public with a series of the most important findings and articles that meet your needs, and facilitate your search for a particular subject.

The series "The most important aspects and characteristic features of the Anunnaki and extraterrestrials" consists of approximately 40 books/booklets, each containing one major topic, which was previously spread out in several books.

*** *** ***

Here is a list of the titles of the 40 books/booklets of the series:

- **Book 1:** You, in the Afterlife, Parallel Dimensions and Beyond the Future of Time and Space.
- **Book 2:** The German UFOs and the supernatural
- **Book 3:** Baalbeck: The Anunnaki's City and Afrit Underground.
- **Book 4:** Anunnaki Genetic Creation of the Human Races, Demons and Spirits.
- **Book 5:** The whole truth about Nibiru "Ne.Be.Ru"-Ashtari: How the Anunnaki live on their planet.
- **Book 6:** The Anunnaki Ba'abs: Stargates.
- **Book 7:** The Anunnaki Ulema Book of Enlightenment: Metaphysical study of the path of wisdom and esoteric knowledge
- **Book 8:** The Anunnaki, Yahweh and God.
- **Book 9:** Abraham and the Anunnaki.
- **Book 10:** St. Tekla, the First Anunnaki Hybrid Christian Saint.
- **Book 11:** 2022, the year the Anunnaki return to Earth.
- **Book 12:** The Anunnaki, Cheribu and Angels on Earth.
- **Book 13:** The Anunnaki classes and categories.
- **Book 14:** Dido, the Anunnaki-Phoenician Princess.

- **Book 15:** The Anunnaki and Enlil.
- **Book 16:** The Anunnaki and Enki.
- **Book 17:** The name the Anunnaki gave you before you were born.
- **Book 17:** The Anunnaki and Fikr.
- **Book 18:** The Anunnaki winged disk and their symbols on Earth.
- **Book 19:** The Anunnaki and the secret esoteric meaning of the mushroom/Holy Grail.
- **Book 20:** The Anunnaki's Conduit and the creation of our brains' cells.
- **Book 21:** Grids and calendar of our lucky hours and days.
- **Book 22:** The Anunnaki Miraya.
- **Book 23:** The Anunnaki and the Hyksos.
- **Book 24:** The Hybrid race from A to Z. Their habitat and lifestyle.
- **Book 25:** Adonis, Dumuzi and the Anunnaki.
- **Book 26:** The supernatural powers of the Anunnaki Ulema.
- **Book 27:** Weapons and black operations of the Grays-Earth Governments Alliance.
- **Book 28:** The Anunnaki Ulema Tarot.
- **Book 29:** The Anunnaki, You, and your double.
- **Book 30:** The Grays from A to Z.
- **Book 31:** The Anunnaki and the vanished civilizations and continents on Earth.
- **Book 32:** Ziggurat and temples of Anunnaki gods in Babylon.
- **Book 33:** The Anunnaki, our genes and the Supersymetric Mind.
- **Book 34:** What the extraterrestrials and the Anunnaki want you to know!
- **Book 35:** Anunnaki symbols, artifacts and cities on Earth.

- **Book 36:** The Anunnaki Chronology from 1,250,000 years ago to the present day. The book includes the genealogical line of descendants and/or remnants of the Anunnaki on Earth, in the regions of Mesopotamia, Babylonia, Sumer, Assyria, Chaldea, Phoenicia, and Turkey.
- **Book 37:** Anunnaki's Akashic Records.
- **Book 38:** The Afarit, Djinns and the Anunnaki.

Note: Four additional books are under preparation.

***   ***   ***

Glossary and Terminology

- **Alal-ra:** A mental channel implanted in the brain by the Anunnaki's geneticists to send and receive information telepathically.

- **Araya:** The domain, the realm, the landscape where 73 different zones of your brain are found. Each zone of the Araya functions differently, because it was created, engineered and programmed differently by the Anunnaki, at the time the prototypes and final "models" of the human race were created. Each zone of the Araya functions differently, because it was created, engineered and programmed differently by the Anunnaki, at the time the prototypes and final "models" of the human race were created.

- **Arka-riyah:** A perfect telepathy.

- **Dou-Kh'oul:** The activation of the Madkhal which is the main entrance of the Ba'ab (Mental-Spatial Stargate).

- **Falak (Dounia):** The world of the human mind. It consists of seven different "Woujoud", meaning existences. Three of these Woujoud already exist in a physical-nonphysical sphere of illusion, called "Kha-Da'h".

- **Fik'r-Ra:** The second Woujoud. It is known to us as the Fifth dimension.

- **Fira-Sah:** The ability to recognize good and evil people.

27

- **Hara-Kiya:** Internal energy.

- **I-Bra.Ah:** Transcending time and space.

- **I-Ka-Ma:** The cleansing or resurrecting the dead within two or three days after they have died.

- **Jaba:** Every thought, each idea you have in your brain, has a vibration. And each vibration occupies a spot in your Araya, called "Jaba". Each Jaba (A hole, so to speak) stores one idea. And each idea or thought in the Jaba of the Araya net produces a vibration.

- **Kadosh-Ra or "Koudous-Ra":** The Sixth dimension.

- **Kha-Da'h:** A physical-nonphysical sphere of illusion.

- **Khalek-Ra:** The fourth Woujoud. It is known to us as the Seventh dimension.

- **Madkhal:** The main entrance of the Ba'ab (Mental-Spatial Stargate).

- **Nafis-Ra:** The first Woujoud. It is known to us as the Fourth dimension.

- **Nis-Ka'h:** Zooming into your Double.

- **Niktat Alkhou-Lood:** The point of the beginning of immortality.

- **Shi-Fa'h:** The act of healing by laying on your hands over the body of a sick person, mentally or physically.

- **Ta.Raa-fou'h:** To be able to levitate and/or bi-locate.

28

- **Tas'sir Fik'ri:** The ability to project one's thoughts into someone else's mind. Also known as the suggestive mental power.

- **Turab** means dirt, sands, carbon, fossils, etc...It is not necessarily clay as we know it today, and as it was alleged or explained by other authors. Some enlightened teachers have said, that Turab or the clay mentioned in the Sumerian texts could also be sea shells. This was mentioned in ancient Phoenicians texts, epics and terracotta.

- **Woujoud:** Existences. Three of these Woujoud already exist in a physical-nonphysical sphere of illusion, called "Kha-Da'h".

*** *** ***

Chapter 1
The Anunnaki Matrix

- The content
- There are three Matrices known to mankind
- Information revealed by the Anunnaki's Matrix
- DNA's fifth unknown element
- Man-made Humans and Reverse Engineering of the Human Brain
- Ba'abs
- Return of the Anunnaki
- A new human race
- The Origin and the Genetic Creation of the Human Races by the Anunnaki.
- The real meaning of the word "Clay" as mentioned in the Sumerian texts
- Contact with extraterrestrials

*** *** ***

31

Chapter 1
The Anunnaki Matrix

The content:
The Anunnaki Matrix is extremely complicated, because it is written in codes, symbols, and geometrical forms. It is a cosmic library, archives, and depository of all the knowledge and events of 15 billions years, the estimated date of the beginning of the known universe.
There are so many fascinating and mind-bending information in this Matrix that have captivated academicians and leading scientists in the Eastern and Western hemispheres.

There are three Matrices known to mankind:
The Anunnaki Matrix is many things indeed.
It is larger than anything the human mind could possibly imagine.
It contains the entire past, present and future of multiple dimensions and civilizations, including planet Earth, and the human races.
There are three Matrices known to mankind:
- 1-The Anunnaki's Matrix,
- 2-The Ulema's Matrix,
- 3-The Humans' Matrix.

Each Matrix has its own dimensions, contents, and scope.
However, the Anunnaki's Matrix includes the Ulema's Matrix, the Ulema's Matrix includes the Humans' Matrix, and the Human's Matrix includes exclusively our habitat on planet Earth.

*** *** ***

33

Information revealed by the Anunnaki's Matrix

There is no way, that in one single book, I could summarize all the data and information of the Anunnaki's Matrix as revealed to the Ulema. It would take millions of volumes.
However, I would like to briefly mention some of the most meaningful revelations of the Matrix as collected and interpreted by the Ulema.

DNA's fifth unknown element:
So far, scientists on Earth have discovered 4 elements in our DNA:
1-Cytosine,
2-Thymine,
3-Adenine,
4-Guanine.

In the Anunnaki's Matrix, there is a fifth element called "I-Bra.Ah", meaning transcending time and space in the Ana'kh language.
The Ulema coined it "Niktat Alkhou-Lood", and it means verbatim: The point of the beginning of immortality. In other words, that fifth element is responsible for an extraordinary longevity of mankind on Earth, and/or its immortality.
It is very possible said an Ulema that after 2022, humans will learn about the secret of immortality, but will never be able to decode the composition and sequences of the fifth element. It would be a catastrophe for humanity and for the future of planet Earth, if humans succeed in decoding the data contained in the fifth element.

Many Ulema are not seriously worried, because with the arrival of the Anunnaki in 2022, the existence of human life and its continuity will be in the hands of the Anunnaki. The Anunnaki explained how this fifth base created the primordial molecules that duplicated themselves and consequently started the life evolution cycles on planet Earth.

It is really mind-boggling. Apparently, scientists in the United States, the United Kingdom and Switzerland are studying this possibility.
They don't say much about their research for obvious reasons. Whistleblowers in American ufology communities are spreading rumors that military scientists and civilian geneticists are conducting advanced experiments on the RNA's fifth base in underground secret military bases in the United States, and at a genetic laboratory in a remote area in Mexico.
These rumors are part of the infernal and phantasmagoric scenario and backdrop of ufology, extraterrestrials' agenda, and conspiracies' theories.
The fifth base has not yet been publicly and officially announced by the scientific community.
But those who have access to privileged sources of information, know very well, that the RNA's fifth base research and studies are an ongoing American secret military-scientific project.

*** *** ***

Man-made humans and reverse engineering of the human brain:
The Ulema said that the Anunnaki's Matrix revealed frightening American scientific progress rotating around the genetic creation of human brains, and the implant of these man-made brains in machines capable of influencing and altering humanity' future and mankind's destiny.
The Anunnaki's Matrix gave the date when these machines will become fully operational: 2021.
The Ulema said that the Anunnaki are not concerned, because their return to Earth in 2022 will annihilate all these machines.

Author's note: American computer guru Ray Kurzweil said: "There will be 32 times more technical progress during the next half century than there was in the entire 20th century, and one of the outcomes is that artificial intelligence could be on a par with human intellect by the 2020s.

35

Machines will rapidly overtake humans in their intellectual abilities and will soon be able to solve some of the most intractable problems of the 21st century..."

In his address to the American Association for the Advancement of Science (AAAS) Dr. Kurzwei portrayed a near future, where machine intelligence will far surpass that of the human brain as they learn how to communicate, teach and replicate among themselves."

Dr. Kurzweil added: "Three-dimensional, molecular computing will provide the hardware for human- level's strong artificial intelligence' by the 2020s. The more important software insights will be gained in part from the reverse engineering of the human brain, a process well under way. Already, more than two dozen regions of the human brain have been modeled and simulated..."
(Noted by Science Daily; AAAS.)

*** *** ***

Ba'abs:
Earth is surrounded by a network of 700 Ba'abs (Stargates). Some of these stargates lead directly to a parallel universe. More information in the book "Ba'ab: The Anunnaki Stargate", published in September 2010.

*** *** ***

Return of the Anunnaki:
The Anunnaki will return to Earth in 2022. Upon their return to Earth, a clash with the Anunnaki is inevitable. This, does not mean that Earth fill fight the Anunnaki.

Anunnaki Ulema Mordechai said verbatim: "People of the Earth will have an unprecedented challenge to face. 2022 is the year of the return of the Anunnaki. And by 2021, governments will commence to release information pertaining to their return." Ulema Saddik added, "Ba'abs will open up, and Anunnaki's stargates will be activated."

*** *** ***

36

A new human race:

A new human race will be created by the Anunnaki starting in 2022. This race is human genetically, but mentally different, because the Conduit will be activated.

One of the coded "Cadrans" of the Anunnaki's Matrix, revealed stunning information and dates about the creation and origin of the human races.

The Anunnaki's Matrix explains how new human species shall be genetically created by them after 2022.

One passage tells how:

a-The Anunnaki in a preliminary stage, will clean human contamination caused by other extraterrestrial races currently living among us. The Zeta Reticulians figure predominantly in the Cadran.

b-The Anunnaki will decide on the fate of humanity through a selection process and the procedures of the ascension to the Ba'abs.

c-The new human race shall not be created from earthly elements.

d-Our physical bodies will disintegrate, and a new DNA will instantly create new fully-grown uncontaminated bodies.

e-A fifth element will be added to the new human DNA.

f-This fifth element will allow the newly created humans to acquire new physical properties-specifications, and mental-scientific capabilities, such as mind transmission, cure for fatal diseases, an extremely extended longevity, and transposition of time-space, meaning the ability to travel to the past and to parallel dimensions.

*** *** ***

The Origin and the Genetic Creation of the Human Races by the Anunnaki.

The real meaning of the word "Clay" as mentioned in the Sumerian texts

The Anunnaki's Matrix mentioned clay as one of the primordial ingredients or elements they have used to create the human race.

37

It is extremely important to understand the real meaning of the word clay.

Clay is NOT what everybody understood or thought to be, from reading the translations of the Sumerian texts.

It is not the earthly clay found in ancient Sumer on the Tigris and Euphrates banks. The Anunnaki's Matrix explained and defined it very very differently. Nevertheless, Judaism, Christianity and Islam got hooked on clay. And scholars who have translated the Sumerian texts and/or interpreted them made a huge mistake when they referred to clay as the mud or dirt substance the Anunnaki found in ancient Iraq, and mixed it with their DNA to create mankind.

*** *** ***

Contact with extraterrestrials:

Planet Earth will have a global contact with other friendly extraterrestrial races by 2022-2023. Although, the Anunnaki are our major and principal link to cosmic civilizations, other extraterrestrial races will enter in communication with us. Such communication will be useful to the human race, because Earth will be invited to explore higher dimensions of science, knowledge and awareness. Such awareness is of a scientific and spiritual nature. Earth will be invited to join a cosmic federation, which gathers highly advanced civilizations which existed in the cosmos for billions of years. The Ba'abs will be activated, and entering parallel dimensions will become a reality.

The Matrix stated that:

- Many of Earth's major religions will disappear by 2022.
- Many cities on Earth are located above negative cosmic currents running beneath the surface of earth.
- The negative energies of those lines cause psychosomatic disturbances and severe illnesses and diseases. Some of those lines are extremely intense under the surface of many cities in the United States.

38

To name a few: Brooklyn, New York, Washington, D.C., Alabama, New Orleans, Louisiana, Nevada. The negative lines can be found around the globe, to name a few: Palestine/Israel, Colombia, Kenya, Nigeria, Greece (Athens and Thessalonica), Jamaica, etc. Positive lines charged with bio-etheric energy are also found in many parts of the globe.

Our homes; the healthy and creative environment we live in:
The Ulema said that in order to create a healthier home environment, the interior of your living-quarters must be in harmony with nature, because your home furniture, interior design and atmosphere influence your psychological state of mind, your emotions, temper, physical and mental health, as well as your relationships with parents, children, neighbors and business.

- The location and placements of ornamental objects, chairs, bookcases, sofas, and every single item inside your home affect the energy flow in your home, and your personal health in your living environment.
- Whether you believe it or not, your rapport with your Double, the development of greater mental faculties, and your peace of mind are greatly influenced by the layout of your home.
- Too much metal and sharp objects inside your home block mental development.
- Too much junk in your home disorient the flux of positive energies.
- To bring serenity to your home, to enhance your mental health, and to develop inspirational and motivational stimuli, your home should have plants, books, windows that welcome the sunlight and fresh air, a small fountain with running water is extremely helpful. Ulema Govinda said, "The presence of pets in your home is very beneficial. Your pets, especially cats, dogs and parrots have psychic abilities, and in many instances, a healing power."

Chapter 2
Death: Is it a philosophical issue?

Chapter 1: Death: Is it a philosophical issue?
- The parallel dimension and frontiers of the after life
- The afterlife does not necessarily begin after we die.
- Your religious beliefs will create illusionary images when you enter the afterlife zone
- Anunnaki Ulema: The righteous people will be reunited with their loved ones including their pets in the afterlife
- The mental punishment is as real as the physical punishment.

- Exclusion from a reunion with loved ones in the afterlife
- Entering a different dimension after you have passed away
- You, the Double and the experience of death.
- What does happen to a deceased person when he/she enters the dimension of the afterlife?
- The Final Judgment and the Cosmic Order "Nizam"
- On the position of a widow meeting multiple husbands in the afterlife
- Question: If Bashar (Humans) can and live for ever in the other world where they reunite with their loved ones, what would be the position, reaction and obligations of a widow who married other men after the death of her first husband, when she meets them afterlife in other dimension?
- Answer
- Eido-Rah: Term for the non-physical substance of a human being's body. In other words, the mental or astral projection of the body leaving earth.
- Hattari: The first stage of the afterlife during the 40 day period following death.

*** *** ***

Chapter 2

Death: Is it a philosophical issue?

Death preoccupied the minds of philosophers, theologians, and spiritists, for centuries. Voluminous books were written on the subject in so many different languages, and according to a multitude of religious beliefs from Tibetan to Hindu, from Egyptian to Phoenician, from Gnosticism to Theosophy, and from Jainism to spiritualism; consequently, death was differently conceived and perceived, and based upon such perceptions, human salvation was divergently and differently defined.

Each religion brings different facets of death and provides particular instruction on how to die, how to guide the departed (Soul, mind and body), and how to reach our final destination. And this destination is of a primordial importance, because it defines and justifies the reason of our existence on Earth.
The Ulema teachings and writings are no exception.
Nevertheless, they are different from the Tibetan, Buddhist, Hindu, Egyptian, Gnostic and organized religions' teachings, dogma, and concepts.
A comparative - even brief – study of those major religious concepts would help us understand how sages and men of wisdom defined the soul, the reason of the creation of mankind, and how finally, our soul reaches the ultimate state of peace, joy and liberation.
The Anunnaki Ulema use the word "Mind", instead.

*** *** ***

43

The parallel dimension and frontiers of the afterlife:

The parallel dimension is so close to us.
The sphere and frontiers of the afterlife begin in the parallel dimension which is so close to us, but we are unable to see it, to feel it and to understand it, because:

1-Our Conduit is not fully activated,
2-We are contaminated by earthy elements,
3-Our mind has not been yet purified,
4-We do not know how to ascend to the Ba'abs,
5-We do not know how to locate Al Madkhal,
6-We have not established a direct rapport with our Double,
7-We have not liberated our mind from physical bondage,
8-We have not freed ourselves from many caprices, lust, greed and attachment to physical possessions.

*** *** ***

The afterlife does not necessarily begin after we die.

In fact, the afterlife does not necessarily begin after we die, because death does not exist; it is simply a transitory stage.
Within our physical world exist so many other worlds. And far away, and deep in the fabric of the universe, distances are reduced, even eliminated, if we zoom into our Double. Matter and anti-matter are de-fragmented in the parallel dimension.
The initiated and enlightened ones can transport themselves to the other world, and visit the far distant corners of the universe through their Double.
Those who are noble in their thoughts, intentions and deeds can accomplish this after an Ulema initiation.

*** *** ***

**Your religious beliefs will create illusionary
images when you enter the afterlife zone.**

If you are a devoted Catholic, you are going to see Jesus or the
Virgin Mary at the end of the tunnel.

If you believe in Krishna, then Krishna will be there, and if you
can't live without watching professional wrestling, Hulk Hogan
will be waiting for you at the end of the tunnel along with all the
creatures of the WrestleMania main event. Take your pick!

Your strong and unconditional religious beliefs as shaped and
influenced by organized religions dictate what are you going to
see in your near-death experience. But those visions happen only
on earth, or while you are suspended between this dimension
and the next one.

But as soon as you cross over, those visions and sensations will
vanish completely, and your strong religious beliefs will dissipate
in thin air.

You will discover a world you have not envisioned before; a
dimension none of your preachers and spiritual advisers ever
understood or explained to you, a universe totally different from
the heaven and hell you read about in the scriptures, because you
will be entering the dimension of the Anunnaki who created you.
It is an immense sphere of so many dimensions, levels and
destinations.

*** *** ***

Anunnaki Ulema: The righteous people will be reunited with their loved ones including their pets in the afterlife.

- The righteous people will be reunited with their loved ones including their pets in the afterlife.
- This reunion will take place in the ethereal Fourth Dimension.
- The reunion is not of a physical nature, but mental. This means, that the mind of the deceased will project and recreate holographic images of people, animals and places.
- All projected holographic images are identical to the original ones, but they are multidimensional.
- Multidimensional means that people, animals and physical objects are real in essence, in molecules, in DNA, and in origin, but not necessarily in physical properties.
- In other words, what you see in the afterlife is real to the mind, but not to your physical senses, because in the after life (In all the seven levels/dimensions of life after death), physical objects, including humans' and animals' bodies acquire different substances, molecular compositions, and new forms.

*** *** ***

46

The mental punishment is as real as the physical punishment.

- The physical rewards and punishments are mental, not physical in nature, but they are as real as the physical ones.
- The deceased will suffer through the mind.
- The pain sensations are real, but are produced by the mind, instead of a physical body. So in concept and essence, the Ulema and Hebraic scholars share similar beliefs; the good person will be rewarded, and the bad person will be punished.
- For the Jews, it is physical, while for the Ulema it is mental, but both reward and punishment are identical in their intensity and application.

*** *** ***

Exclusion from a reunion with loved ones in the afterlife

- The wicked will not be indefinitely excluded from a reunion with loved ones.
- The wicked will remain in a state of loneliness, chaos, confusion and mental anguish for as long it takes to rehabilitate him/her.
- This state of punishment and rehabilitation can last for a very long period of time in an uncomfortable sphere of existence inhabited by images of frightening entities created by the mind as a form of punishment.
- Some scholars and ethicists believe that the projection of these macabre and scary entities are created by the subconscious of the wicked person.

47

- Other scholars believe that the holographic imageries are produced by the Double housing the mind.
- Eventually, all wicked persons will reunite with their loved ones after a long period of purification and severe punishment.
- Soul is a metaphysical concept created by Man.
- Soul is a religious idea created by humans to explain and/or to believe in what they don't understand.
- It is more accurate to use the word Mind instead.
- The mind thinks and understands. The soul does not, perhaps it feels, if it is to be considered as a vital force and source of feelings in your physical body.
- In the afterlife, such source of feelings is non-existent, and in the dimensions of the after world, such source is useless.

*** *** ***

Entering a different dimension while you are still alive

Excerpts from the readings of the Honorable Sheik Al Mutawalli, verbatim, word for word. Translated according to the original reading, and preserving its authentic caché.

*** *** ***

In this life: Preparing yourself to enter the other world while you are still alive

- On earth, in this limited physical dimension, our supernatural powers are limited. They are governed by the laws of physics that define and regulate the nature, substance and functions of our planet.
- However, the mind can escape from the earthly bondage and Earth's physical frontiers, and enter different dimensions.
- The ultimate guide for that journey is the astral body. In the past, we called it the double. In this particular situation, it is wiser to call it your guide, because during your journey to the other world - not afterlife yet - your physical body will remain on Earth, and there is no body *per se* to refer to.
- No physical substance can enter non-physical sphere.
- No human voice can reach the ear of non-physical entities.
- No human voice or any sound produced on Earth is heard in other dimensions.
- However, your guide (Your Double) carries within itself everything that constitutes your physical body, including memory, thoughts and introspection. But not physical sensations and corporal feelings.

49

- While your physical body is still quite alive but dormant in the physical surroundings (It could be your home, your office, your car, etc.), your Double retains all the faculties your brain and body received at the moment of your birth.
- Of course, your knowledge will increase considerably throughout the ages as you enter school, colleges, universities, and as you begin to learn from your teachers and tutors. We call this kind of knowledge "Earth's Knowledge".
- What you did not know is, that your "Conduit" which is located in the cells of your brains contains an enormous amount of knowledge you did not tap in yet, because you were not aware of its existence, or because you have never believed in the existence of your "Conduit".
- The Conduit consists of ultra-microscopically small tissues and membranes in your brain's cells. They are infinitesimally small, no microscopes can detect them.
- This Conduit contains and retains everything your creator put in you, in your body, and in your mind. Only "Al Mounawarin" (Enlightened Ones) can tap into the Conduit. (Author's note: The Anunnaki have similar Conduit).
- Once the Conduit is activated by your teacher, you, (the student) become "Mounawar" (Enlightened).

Note: Mounawar is the singular of Mounawarin.

- Without an activated "Conduit" you cannot communicate with your "Double".
- And the way you communicate with your Conduit is via telepathy.
- Telepathy is not reading others' minds. Telepathy is not channeling. Telepathy is one of the tools you must use to be on the same vibrational level or frequency of your Double.
- Your double is made out of electromagneticectoplasma substance. It has electricity, magnetism, plasma and ethereal energy called "Rouh".

- The Rouh is the non-physical image projection of what you are if you were separated from your body.
- For now, forget everything about your body. Do not worry about it. No harm is going to happen to your body. It will stay where it is, only your "Other Self" will change. Once, your Conduit is activated - better to say open – your mind begins to see new things...no, you are not hallucinating at all... you are only experiencing and seeing new things, called "Rou'yah" (Visions).
- The very first thing you will see is absolutely nothing. It is like if you were looking at an empty world without buildings, cars, trees and people.
- For a few seconds, you will be confused. Your mind is still working. But your mind cannot understand yet this emptiness.
- In fact, it is not emptiness at all. There is no such thing as emptiness or empty space or nothingness in the world. Everything is part of something else.
- Because your mind is seeing something very new, or because your mind is seeing nothing at all, for now, that is, your mind cannot explain to you what "Is This?" What are you experiencing? Where are you? In this state, you will be confused, but it is not going to last long.
- Your brain is reprogramming itself (Note: The Honorable teacher did not use the word "Programming", but that is the most *a propos* word I can use to explain to you what he meant. The word he used is "Takarub". It means getting closer to...
- In a very short time, your mind will be self-reprogrammed, because it is in the process of acquiring a "Memory". In this memory, are stored all the knowledge and data that allow your mind to understand what you are seeing. Almost 85% of your "Other-Self" is made out of memory in the astral world, contrary to what other schools of thoughts and religions claim.
- I will recapitulate: Your Conduit is open now.
- Your mind has found a rich memory full of information.

51

- The vision of nothingness or emptiness vanishes. Now you begin to see something new. It starts like this:

*** *** ***

This is what you will see first, when you enter the other world

1-Many layers of light dispersed as wide, and as far as you can see.

2-The shades appear fourth dimensional.

3-You are acquiring now an extra visual dimension. There are no words I can use for now to describe this new Fourth dimension. Anyhow, you will not be able to understand it no matter how hard I try to explain this to you. But in due time, you will understand.

4-Slowly slowly and very gradually you begin to see yourself; an image of yourself.

5-You get scared. It is understandable. This is your first reaction...fear!

6-Your mind will readjust itself, and in a blink of an eye, your fear will dissipate.

7-Your mind is telling you now that you are no longer on earth.

8-Your mind will reassure you that you are safe and no physical harm will come to you, because you are pure mind, but this mind is the ultimate reality.

9-Your Double will stand straight, right before your eyes.

10-And all of a sudden, faster than the speed of light, you're zoomed into your Double.

11-Your Double and "You" are united. From now on, there are no more "You", the person who lived on earth, and the other one (Your Double) that lives in the other dimension.

You become one with "all of yourselves", one existence, one entity; an ethereal, astral, mental person.

12-You begin to float. How? It does not matter. You are floating now. Where? So close and so near to everything you knew and saw on earth.

Yet, you are not physical. Your Double looks exactly like you on the outside. It has the external physical looks of the body you had on earth, but it is transparent, and light like ether.

And you are in full control of this new body.

13-You will be able to remember all the places you have visited, all the things you liked and disliked. You will be able to visit any part of the world instantly.

13-You might experience strange feelings, such as falling so fast toward earth or an abyss, or being suspended in air and you don't know what to do next. But in seconds, those feelings will fade away. And you continue to enjoy everything you are seeing and what you can do next.

14-Some like to go back and visit their body; the one they left on earth. In fact, many do. Try it. Just command your new body to take you there. And there you are hovering over your body. You begin to gaze at your body. Irresistibly you come closer to your physical body laying there motionless.

And a new sensation invades you; you pity this mortal, weak, motionless, insignificant piece of flesh and bones. And all of a sudden, you understand that your physical body has a minimal value. And you will realize, that what really counts is your mind.

Note: Those who are interested in learning more about this subject are encouraged to read my other book "Ulema: Code and Language of the World Beyond."

*** *** ***

Entering a different dimension after you have passed away.

According to the Anunnaki Ulema life continues after the so-called death. They have explained in their teachings that human life does not end on earth.
Although the physical body decays, the mind continues to live in another dimension.

The Judeo-Christian-Muslim tradition uses "soul" instead of mind. The Ulema believe that the soul is one of the many manifestations of the mind, although the soul does not manifest itself in any form or shape, not even in an etheric or ethereal sense. Buddhism also uses mind instead of soul.

Excerpts from the readings of the Honorable Sheik Al Mutawalli, verbatim, word for word. Translated according to the original reading, and preserving its authentic caché.

- At the very moment, your body expires (At the moment of your death), your Double instantly separates itself from the sphere surrounding your body.
- Your Double that co-existed with you in your physical dimension was never physically attached to your body.
- In many instances, sometimes for a very long period, your "Double" has remained distant from your physical body for many reasons. But in general, your "Double" stays very close to you. The distance separating your Double from your physical body depends on your health condition.
- It is very healthy and even necessary to keep your Double at a close proximity of your body.

54

- Miraculous recoveries are sometimes attributed to divine intervention.
- Sudden recoveries are sometimes attributed to a strong will and one's determination to be healthy again. And of course, there are other inexplicable recoveries which are attributed to other inexplicable events and phenomena. Everything is possible. But the main reason for a sudden and inexplicable recovery is the sudden re-entry of your healthy Double in your physical body. It reactivates and energizes everything in your body. It is like recharging a dead battery.
- Your Double knows very well how your body functions, far more and better than any physician. Because the physical condition of your body at the time you relinquish your last breath is paramount, the passage to another dimension is henceforth influenced and altered accordingly.
- For example, people who die in a brutal accident or commit suicide, their Double becomes instantly impaired and dysfunctional at the time of their death. Suicide is wrong.
- No matter how miserable is your life, you should never commit suicide. Tragic death and suicide confuse and disorient your Double.
- Disorienting your Double is harmful to your mind. And because your mind is your vehicle to the other world, you should avoid anything or anyone that could cause you a tragic, painful and sudden death. The body has its wounds. The mind has wounds too, but you can't see them. Your Double does.
- If you leave earth in that condition, your mind will not lead you toward the Ba'ab. You will be disoriented. If you have not caused your own death, but suffered a lot at the time of your death, and your Double was far away from you, your passage to the other world will not be pleasant at all. And the Ba'ab will not be open right away to allow you to enter the other side of the world.

- Of course, eventually you will pass through, but not before 40 tumultuous and painful days you will spend lost and confused in the realm of confusion and loneliness.
- In normal situation such as a death of a natural cause, the passage to the other world takes its normal course, at the end of the Double's self-judgment and assessment of deeds, actions and thoughts of the deceased.

*** *** ***

You, the Double and the Experience of Death. What does happen to a deceased person when he/she enters the dimension of the afterlife?

- At the moment of death, he will be guided by his Double to a neutral sphere where he will spend 40 days of purification.
- During those 40 days, he will receive guidance and orientation from his "Double".
- Because he was not a bad person, at the end of the 40 days period, and right before going through the Ba'ab, he will be allowed to revisit the living he wishes to see one more time. Also, he will be permitted to hover over places he wishes to visit for the last time.
- In some instances, the visited parents of the deceased feel his last apparition to them. Usually, the deceased appears to them in an ethereal form. It is not totally ectoplasmic, because at that stage, the deceased has already lost all the physical properties of his body. So his apparition is mental holography.
- The apparition does not last long. It fades way within a few seconds. And this is the last message (Sort of a Farewell), the parents will receive from him/her.
- After that last visit, no contact will ever occur again between the dead person and his/her loved ones. His/her mind (Soul to others) will leave earth for ever.
- Do not be duped by those who claim, that they can contact the dead and communicate with the spirits.
- Be aware of those fake spirits' séances and channeling. Unless, the mind (Soul or Spirit to others) initiates a contact during particular stages, no living being on earth can communicate with the dead.
- Contact with dead people is possible, if the enlightened one has been granted the privilege to go through the Al Madkhal and the Ba'ab.

- On the last day of the 40 days period, the deceased is zoomed into his/her Double, and becomes one with his "Original Form".
- The Original Form is what it created him/her. This is why we call it Double.
- The Double is the real persona of the human being. Everything we have in our body and mind came from our Double.
- Even though, some of our mental and physical faculties and properties are usually damaged on earth for various reasons, such as illness, malnutrition, fear, prejudices, tortures, confusion, etc., the original faculties in our Double are immune, because the physical cannot affect the non-physical, nor reach any dimension beyond the "Zinar" (Belt of Earth).
- As soon as the deceased becomes one with the Double, the mind enters the Ba'ab on its way to the Fourth dimension.
- The Fourth dimension is a sphere so close to earth. And because the mind of the deceased in this dimension is capable of mental and spatial dilatation, quite often, the mind and the perimeter of the fourth dimension extend like an echo.
- It is through the extension of that echo, that contacts with the fourth dimension's inhabitants are possible, but they are so rare. Almost, they never happen.
- Once, the mind (The deceased or visiting entity) enters the Fourth dimension, the deceased begins to see all sorts of things, shapes, colors, entities, human forms, spiritual forms created by his/her memory. It is a very pleasant sphere consisting of only good sensations, a sense of tranquility and safety.
- From now on, we will never again feel pain, sorrow, fatigue...no more worries, frustration and anxiety.
- Yet, the Fourth dimension is not a perfect dimension, even though we are reunited with friends and beloved ones, even our pets, for we have to progress and reach a higher dimension.

58

- The Fifth dimension is better and prettier. And within it, there are so many other worlds of an unimaginable beauty, and so many wonderful things to see and do...

*** *** ***

The Final Judgment and the Cosmic Order "Nizam"

- The "Nizam" (Cosmic Order and Law) tells us, that nobody escapes the final judgment. Each one of us is responsible for his/her acts, deeds, thoughts, even intentions. The principle of accountability is "Da.Em" (Perpetual).
- Eventually, all people will be saved at the end.
- There is no such thing as hell where human flesh and bones are burned by an eternal fire.
- Through the Ba'ab, the good person will be admitted to the grace and beauty of a higher dimension of happiness and peace. The bad person will not be allowed to enter the Ba'ab right away.
- When a bad person dies, he immediately faces his Double. In this instance, the Double acts as a conscience and as a judge.
- The entire life flashes before his mind as a holographic sequence of events, deeds and thoughts. It is a large screen of his entire life.
- Everything he did in his life on earth is projected on this screen.
- Because he was a bad person, he will not be allowed to enter the Madkhal (Entrance to the other world). His double will stop him right there.
- He will be punished according to the gravity of his acts and thoughts. This bad person could spend thousands of years in a state of confusion, loneliness, fear, anguish, mental pain and suffering.
- The mental pain is as real and as atrocious as a physical pain.
- There is no escape.

60

- The bad person will spend those very long years in a sphere inhabited by chaos, horrific entities and psychosomatic pain, even though, he does no longer possess a physical body.
- All the properties of his physical bodies are transferred to his mind in this new sphere , and as a result, he will suffer physically through his mind.
- And as a punishment, he will feel the same pain and suffering he caused to others. As I told you before, there is no physical hell in the afterlife. But as I see it, this sort of punishment is more painful than burning in fire.
- Because his Double is partially responsible, the Double will suffer too. Consequently, the deceased bad person will not be united with his Double.
- The separation between the deceased bad person and his Double will last for many years, as long as it takes to rehabilitate him and purify his past deeds and thoughts.
- Once the rehabilitation is complete, and the bad person has been totally purified, he unites with his Double and loses his psychological (Psychosomatic) senses of the physical properties of his body. Thus the pain ceases.
- From the Madkhal he reaches the Ba'ab that takes him to a higher dimension; a sphere of tranquility, beauty, and eternal peace.
- However, this sphere is not perfect, because it is the lowest of the seven other dimensions that constitute the final and eternal destinations of the human existence.
- As we progress mentally (Spiritually to others), we reach higher and higher dimensions.
- The highest sphere we can reach is the Six dimension.
- The Seventh dimension is the "Malakout" (Almost same word in Hebrew, Aramaic, Phoenician, Syriac and Arabic, Ana'kh, and it means kingdom or paradise), where the Supreme Energy (God or the Original Force of Creation) originated, exists, lives, and extends infinitely.

*** *** ***

61

On the position of a widow meeting multiple husbands, in the afterlife.

Question: If Bashar (Humans) can live for ever in the other world where they reunite with their loved ones, what would be the position, reaction and obligations of a widow who married other men after the death of her first husband, when she meets them afterlife in other dimension?

Answer:
- Since we do believe that life continues after death, multiple marriages could cause a state of mental confusion, and perhaps embarrassment for the deceased widow who remarried after the death of the departed spouse...this could happen upon meeting multiple husbands or wives in the early stage in the Fourth dimension. But once the Mind is purified, and as we progress mentally and spiritually, we begin to see and understand the situation very differently...
- In higher dimensions...afterlife, the Mind functions, sees and understands things very very differently from the way we were accustomed to on earth.
- The deceased continues to live after death as a Mind.
- The Mind retains terrestrial memory, even though the Mind has lost all sensorial properties.
- The Mind cannot alter the past. We are stuck with the memory of everything we have done on earth. Only the Anunnaki who created us genetically can alter the past of the person they have created. And by altering the past, the Anunnaki can erase all kinds of memories, including related events that occurred in one particular dimension.
- This is applicable only when a person has been created on earth by an Anna.Ki (Anunnaki).

62

- I said on earth, because there are so many different beings who were created by other creators governing other planets, stars and dimensions.
- It is a very unique story with human beings and animals who live on earth. On our planet, we multiply through "Mouda-Ja'ah" (Intercourse).
- On other planets, reproduction is done through different processes and methods; no physical contacts or sexual acts are necessary.
- Thus, there are no physical attachments, no corporal desire, and no sense of being physically possessed by another person, or committed to a physical partner.
- The collective mind of the community on some other planets substitutes for sexual desires, lust for the flesh, and corporal pleasures.
- Because humans can reach immortality in other dimensions starting in the Fifth dimension, freeing ourselves from physical memories is essential; this is done in the Fourth dimension.
- Once the purification is complete, and as soon as the process of freeing ourselves from past corporal memories is done, the Mind readjusts itself accordingly. This means, that almost everything we loved or treasured on earth, such as wealth, owning a luxurious car, properties, nice wardrobe, sexual pleasures, etc., become meaningless and shallow.
- This is why, we, the human beings...we are the lowest form of living entities in the universe, and our habitat "Ard" (Planet Earth) is lowest form of habitat in the universe. This decadence is caused by greed, violence, egoism, betrayal, and sexual bondage.
- Now, we go back to the deceased who is meeting the multiple spouses he/she had after the death of the first partner in life. The deceased will not feel embarrassed at all, because the Mind in the afterlife, once it has been purified, begins to understand that physical attachment causes sorrow and grief.

63

- And because there are no more sexual desires in the afterlife, these desires lose their meaning and importance.
- Consequently, the position of the deceased widow who is now pure Mind changes completely. Multiple spouses are no longer looked upon as multiple spouses, because they have acquired different nature and composition, and the association of the Mind with their physical properties on earth is integrated into the collective mind of the community.
- Thus, all of them will continue to live, think, and interact with each other as a continuous sequence of the chain of immortality free of physical attachment.

***   ***   ***

Eido-Rah:

Term for the non-physical substance of a human being's body. In other words, the mental or astral projection of the body leaving earth. Eido-Rah manifests to human beings, and particularly to the parents of the deceased person during a period of less than 40 days, following the death of a relative.

From Eido-Rah, derived the Greek word Eidolon (A phantom).

According to the scribes of the Book of Rama-Dosh: "After we die, the primordial source of energy in our body leaves our body. This energy is a substance made out of Fik'r closely connected and attached to a copy of ourselves preserved in the Fourth dimension, which is not very far away from us, and from Earth. As soon as this energy leaves the physical body, the mind of the deceased becomes confused instantly. The mind does not realize that the body is dead. At this particular stage, the mind is unable to realize right away that it has entered a new dimension.

Although this new dimension is identical to the one we live in and what we call Earth, it is also very different because time, space and distance no longer exist. And also because, it exists at a different vibrational level.

64

Everything becomes meta-linear.

Because the mind is confused, it tries to return to Earth. The first places, the mind (Or the new form-substance of the deceased one) searches for, and/or tries to return to, are always the familiar places on Earth, such as home, office, recreation center, church, mosque, synagogue, temple, etc...but the most sought place is usually home.

So, the deceased person returns home for a very short period. This does not happen all the time. Only when the deceased person is totally confused and disoriented.

First, the deceased tries to contact relatives and close parents.

When the deceased begins to realize that parents and relatives are not responding, the deceased tries again to send messages telepathically.

Some messages if intensified can take on ectoplasmic forms, or appear as a shadow usually on smooth substances such as mirror and glass.

Some deceased people will keep on trying to contact their beloved ones left behind for a period of 39 days and 11 hours. After this time, the deceased dissipates, and no further attempts to establish contact with the living are made."

In another passage from the Book of Ramadosh, we read (Verbatim):

"Although, it is impossible to reach the deceased one as soon as he/she leaves the body, and/or during the 39 days and 11 hours period following his death, sometimes, if we are lucky, and/or were extremely attached to the person we lost, a short contact with him or with her is still possible if we pay attention to unusual things happening around us. Those unusual things are difficult to notice, unless we pay a great attention. They happen only once, sometimes twice, but this is very rare..." The book provides techniques and methods pertaining to all forms and means of such contact.

*** *** ***

65

Hattari:

The first stage of the afterlife during the 40 day period following death. In that stage, a new life-form develops in the mind of deceased people. A brief description of Hattari was given by a lady (Who apparently was an Ulema) to her beloved son.

Here is an excerpt from the "Book of Ramadosh", and from the Book "On the Road to Ultimate Knowledge: The Anunnaki-Ulema Extraterrestrial Tao", co-authored by Dr. Ilil Arbel, and Maximillien de Lafayette:

The scene is between Germain Lumiere, an Ulema from France who has just lost his mother.

It appeared later on, that his mother was an Ulema too, but she has never told him that, for reasons we don't know.

Two days after she passed away in Paris, his mother appeared to him during her funeral, as she has promised him.

The young Ulema asked his mother lots of question about the after-life, and what is she doing there. Herewith, a brief excerpt from their conversation:

Location: Cemetery of Père-Lachaise, Paris, France.

Time: In the afternoon, during the funeral of Countess....mother of Germain.

Personages:

1-The deceased mother appears as a spirit and talks to her son Germain, while her physical body is in the coffin.

2-Germain in tears talking to his dead mother for the last time.

3-Sylvie: She is Germain's sister.

Excerpt below: Germain is telling us what they talked about at the funeral.

"I returned to Mama, who was looking sadly at Sylvie. It's really too bad I can't talk to her," Mama said to me, "but some day, of course, she will know, like everyone else. Ah, well, let's go to the more secluded areas. We don't want people to think you are talking to yourself."

We wandered around the cemetery. Père Lachaise, is one of the most beautiful cemeteries in the world, full of trees, impressive statues, and old tombstones. Shady lanes provided privacy, and we could talk freely.

"So tell me about your experience in the Afterlife, Mama," I said.

"I have not been there very long, you know, but time and space play a different role there, and also, my training allows me to know what it is really like and what will happen next," said Mama. "You will also know, when the time comes."

"Doesn't everyone know?"

"No, many of the dead don't realize that they are dead. They don't seem to see the border between life and afterlife. These people can be very anxious.

They sometimes try to get back to Earth, meet their loved ones, and they are very upset when the living cannot see them."

"So what happens to them?"

"The guides, spirits of higher dimensions, help them realize that they are dead. Sometimes, if persons have a real need to go back to Earth to accomplish something, the guides are saddened by their pain, and allow them to go back, manifest, and complete their task. Once they do that, they can come back, much happier and calmer. It only happens once, of course, but after that they are ready to adjust to the afterlife."

"What is it like, over there? Were you scared when you passed on?"

"There is nothing frightening about the afterlife," said Mama. "It is very much like earth, but peaceful, much more beautiful, and there is no strife or violence of any kind. To the departed, who have shed their bodies and are occupying a new body, it is as physical as the earth is to the living. Everyone is healthy, there is no disease, no pain, no violence.

There are cities with streets and buildings, gardens and parks, countryside – all seems normal, like a poetic interpretation of life. What you see here is visual projections.

You see millions of real people, coming and going in huge waves. There is much to do, since the place you come to first is no more than a quick stop. You only stay here for twenty to thirty days, some times forty days, and then move on."

"Do they know where they are going?"

"It depends. Most people cannot see what is ahead of them, only what is behind them. But they always move on to a higher phase."

"So naturally they are a bit scared of the unknown."

"Yes, some of them experience anxiety. That is what the twenty to thirty days period is for, deciding what needs and things to be done. And they are helped by the guides, or by people who chose to stay longer in this place."

"So you can stay there longer?"

"Yes, there are various options, of course. One option is to go to the place you have created when you built your "Minzar" and planned a place of rest and happiness.

Many people choose to go there for a while – it is up to them how long they would stay there. Time is not really a very important issue where we are.

It seems to me that time has stopped. You can stay there forever if you like it very much."

"The place created with the Minzar must be very appealing to most people, I should say," I said. "It's custom made for your own happiness."

"Yes, and the person already has friends, a place to stay, things to do, anything he or she likes best. It's a good option. But eventually, I would say one should try to evolve into the higher dimensions. You don't know what you miss unless you see it."

"When I built the Minzar, Rabbi Mordechai told me that I could not stay in the place I created for too long, since the energy would dissipate and the living body will call me back. But I suppose it's different when one is dead."

"Yes, since this is now part of the depot of knowledge located in your brain, which was created by the Minzar experience. It is your Spatial Memory, my son."

"So you plan to move on after the thirty days?"

"Yes. It is as it should be, and I want to evolve into the higher dimensions. But as I promised, I will come back for you and be your guide when it is your time to follow me.

Think about it as a short, though necessary separation, but temporary all the same. What it all comes down to, Germain, is that there is no death.

And the afterlife offers so many opportunities for new growth, new knowledge. There is nothing to fear."

"Will you see Papa? Will I see him when I go there?"

"Of course we will. Do not worry and do not mourn me, Germain."

"I will try not to, Mama. I promise."

"Well, my son, I will be leaving now. No need to say goodbye. Rather, au revoir."

I closed my eyes, not wishing to see her leave, and felt something brush my cheek as if she kissed me. When I opened my eyes, there was no sign of her. She was gone.
I went home and helped Sylvie attend to the visitors; I have never felt so numb."

*** *** ***

Chapter 3
The Astral Body
"Your Double"

How your "Double" can affect your life, success and development

- The Ulema Eastern teachings and writings
- Question: Then what's next? What is happening now to the two bodies; the physical and non-physical at the time we are conceived?
- Answer
- Question: Does our double interact with us while we are small babies?
- Answer
- Question: Why these moments are precious in our lives?
- Answer
- Question: Can we communicate with our "Astral Body"?
- Answer
- First Situation: When your Double appears on its own
- Second Situation: You initiate the contact with your Double
- Entering a different dimension while you are still alive
- In this life: Preparing yourself to enter the other world while you are still alive
- This is what you will see first, when you enter the other world

- Entering a different dimension after you have passed away
- You, the Double and the Experience of Death
- What does happen to a deceased person when he/she enters the dimension of the afterlife?

*** *** ***

Chapter 3
The Astral Body
"Your Double"

How your "Double" can affect your life, success and development

The "Double" is a western term used to represent your other body that exists in the astral dimension. The "other body" is a replica of your physical body. The truth is, your physical body is a "physical projection" and a replica of your original body that existed before you were born.

It is not so easy to explain this notion using ordinary words. Ulema teachers have their own terminology, but I will try to simplify the matter as much as I can.

If you were born in the West, and you have developed an interest in spiritual subjects, you probably have already read about the astral body. In the United States of America, there is an immense interest in the occult, metaphysics and Eastern religions. Consequently, a vast literature on the subject is available to the readers.

But for some reason, the nature and attributes of "Astral Double" were described very differently from the way spiritualists and Ulema described them in their Eastern teachings, readings (Kira'at), and manuscripts. To add more inaccuracy, the Western writers put on their own spin.

*** *** ***

73

The Ulema Eastern teachings and writings:

In the Middle and Near East, the "Astral Body" or simply your "Double" and its properties are explained by the Ulema as follows:
From the readings "Kira'at" of honorable Sheik Al Mutawalli.

Note: At the end of this section, excerpts from Western writings about the Astral Body are provided for analogy purposes. Also, metaphysical instruction on how to communicate with your "Double" and how to use its hidden powers to your advantage are provided by the Ulema.

*** *** ***

• Before you were born, and before your body took shape, YOU (as a human being) have existed somewhere as an idea.
• What is this idea? We will give you an example. Before a product is mass produced, inventors and artists design and create a model or a prototype of each product. And everything begins with the drawing board.
• On this board, shape, form, dimensions, colors and specifications of the product are defined and illustrated. It started with an idea.
• The idea became a project and the project found its existence on the drawing board. In fact, everything in life started with an idea, continued with a sketch before it reached its final form, and eventually the market.
• Your physical body is a perfect product. And this product came from an idea like everything that has been created. Nothing comes from nothing.
• Who came up with this idea?
• This depends on your religious beliefs. If you believe in the Judeo-Christian tradition, then, your God is the originator of this idea. He created the first draft of your physical body on his drawing board. Most certainly, God had to think about how your body should look like.

- On the Judeo-Christian drawing board of the creation of mankind, God decided how the physical body should come to life. You are much more important than a commercial product or a commodity like a car, or a soda bottle.
- The designers, artists and engineers at the automobile factory and plant spent many hours designing the model of the car, and the manufacturers of the soda bottle spent some good time going through various designs of the shapes and looks of bottles before they chose the most suitable design for their product.
- Now, if you think that you are more important than a car or a bottle, then, it is logical to assume that somebody has spent some time designing you, otherwise, you will surface as a non-studied and not well-researched product.
- If you look at your body very carefully, you will find out that your body is an extremely complicated machine and your brain consists of a very intricate wiring system that requires an engineer or at least a first class designer.
- In summary, you did not come right away without a plan, without a well-thought design, and without an idea that created the design and execution of your physical body.
- At the very beginning and early stage of the creation of your physical body, the "Divine" or "Superior" architect-engineer conceived your physical looks as a picture in the astral world.
- And the astral world for now call it: The World of Ideas; a non-physical world.
- In a non-physical world, everything is non-physical, it is astral, it is ethereal.
- When the ethereal image or idea becomes reality and adopts physical properties like eyes, legs, feet and bones, this idea or your "prototype" becomes a physical body and enters the physical world via the womb of your mother.

- Yet, it remains deeply and directly connected to the draft of the first copy of your physical body.
- And since the first draft of your non-physical body and your recently acquired physical body (or about to be developed in the womb of your mother) are still connected to each other, both bodies (The Idea or Draft and your physical body) co-exist.
- The physical body is inside your mother, and the non-physical body called double or first body exists outside the physical world.
- So, the other copy, or more precisely the first copy of You is called your "Double". And where is this non-physical world? It is in the mind of your creator and on his/her drawing board.

*** *** ***

Question: Then what's next? What is happening now to the two bodies; the physical and non-physical at the time we are conceived?

Answer:
As soon as you begin to develop as a small physical body (a small fetus) inside the womb of your mother, the idea or draft that created you before you entered the womb of your mother begins to feed your brain's cells and program your intellect.

In other words, your brain begins to receive all the information and characteristics that will create and define your personality, temper, character, persona and nature. During the very first 40 days, everything your "Creator" wanted you to be or become start to "go inside your brain" and in the physiology of your body.
And during this very critical intellectual and physical formation, the other aspect of you, your Double, enters a dimension very close to your mother, and once your mother delivers you, your double, the non-physical body will leave the "surroundings" of your mother and follow you.

From this moment, your Double will stay with you until you die.

*** *** ***

Question: Does our double interact with us while we are small babies?

Answer:
Yes.

It interacts with us in a most fascinating way, noticeable only to the "small child we are", and not to the others. Many children have seen their double. And many of them spoke to their double, and played with their double.

In many instances, children called their double "my friend", or "a friend who came to visit me."

Unfortunately, many parents discouraged their small children from talking about their "imaginary friends", or fantasizing about the visits of their unseen friends."

This is very common. Ulema children are encouraged to talk about their "imaginary friends".

These are very precious moments in our lives.

*** *** ***

Question: Why these moments are precious in our lives?

Answer:
Because during this stage, the infant and later on, the small child, has a direct access to his/her double. If the child is deprived from this contact, the Double could dissipate for ever. Of course, in the future, the Double might appear again on certain occasions.

But, because we have lost touch with our Double, and we no longer remember the beautiful and friendly visits of our forgotten imaginary friends, our mind and common sense will automatically dismiss the sudden apparition of our Double as a reality.

77

In these instances, people quite often say: "I am seeing things", or "Am I hallucinating?"

Therapists will rush so quickly to explain the phenomenon as a trick by the mind. It is not a trick at all. It just happened that your Double is paying you a visit. Instead of questioning your sanity, you must rejoice and welcome your "friend".

In fact, your Double is the most truthful, caring and best friend you ever had, simply because it is YOU!

Your Double appeared to you for many reasons. Your "double" always watches over you. It cares about you.

Its presence is a sign of friendship, sometimes necessary and indispensable for solving your problems and finding a way to get out of trouble. You should welcome your Double and listen to.

*** *** ***

Question: Can we communicate with our "Astral Body"?

Answer:
The initiated ones can; it is a matter of learning, practice and patience. However, you have to remember, that the living cannot contact the dead. By reaching the sphere of your Double or Astral Body, you are reaching yourself, not a dead substance, a departed entity or a spirit.

Untrained persons cannot contact their Double, but can be trained and taught by the Ulema. And the training has nothing to do with magic, spiritism or religious trances and state of ecstasy. It is purely mental, intellectual, and scientific.

Here, we will be talking about two situations:

A- First situation: Your Double materializes before you on its own,

B- Second situation: You initiate the contact with your Double.

First Situation: When your Double appears on its own

Sometimes, the Astral Body materializes before you eyes, even though you did not try to contact it.

This apparition has many meanings, and could be interpreted differently according to the circumstances.

Sometimes, your Double appears to you to warn you against an imminent danger. Sometimes, to guide you in a moment of despair and difficulties.

Some other times, when you "see yourself" as a fragile ectoplasmic thin substance like a fog for instance, your Double apparition is telling you, that a very important event is going to happen and it could change the course of your life.

In rare instances, this apparition could mean that your days are numbered. Short after Lord Byron saw his Double he passed way.

Second Situation: You initiate the contact with your Double

Now, you are trying to contact your Double. You initiate the contact. If you are not one of the enlightened persons, you would not know what to do, and where to start. Like everything in the universe, including speeches and lectures...everything begins with an introduction and ends with an epilogue.
This is the right path. In contacting your Double, you must have an introduction that comes in the form of an entry or entrance into the "Al-Madkhal".

Al Madkhal is a state of mind that leads you toward the Ba'ab.
In the Ulema vocabulary, Al Madkhal means verbatim: Entrance and/or where you step in.
Ba'ab is a spatial place that exists around the physical dimension of our world. In the Anunnaki-Ulema vocabulary, Ba'ab means verbatim: Door.
And from and through this door you enter the other dimension where your Astral Body (Your Double) exists. In the West, ufologists, and even space scientists nickname "Ba'ab stargate.
It is not totally correct, because to them, stargate is a gate through which spaceships can travel through the infinity of space and conquer space-time, thus reducing the enormous distances between stars and planets, and reaching destinations in the universe at a speed greater than the speed of sound and light.
For the Ulema, the Ba'ab can be used as a spatial stargate, and a mental means to reach the non-physical world as well; no spaceships are needed to communicate with your Double.

*** *** ***

Chapter 4
Learning from our Double

- Learning from our Double and acquiring supernatural faculties
- Zooming into your Double and acquiring Anunnaki's supernatural faculties
- Question: A novice asked the teacher this question: What do we get from zooming into our Double?
- Contacting the dead through your Double
- Question: A novice asked the teacher these questions: Can we contact our departed parents through our double? And is it dangerous to contact the dead?
- The Theosophy view
- Excerpts from the honorable Ulema's answer to the question: Can we contact our departed parents through our double? And is it dangerous to contact the dead?
- Question: A novice asked the teacher this question: What do we get from zooming into our Double?
- Learning how to communicate with your Double
- Talking to my teacher

***   ***   ***

81

Chapter 4
Learning from our Double and acquiring supernatural faculties

The following is taken from a Kira'a by an Ulema, dialogues with students, and an honorable teacher's answers to questions by novices.

Zooming into your Double and acquiring Anunnaki's supernatural faculties

Question
A novice asked the teacher this question: What do we get from zooming into our Double?

Answer of the honorable Ulema:

- The initiated and enlightened ones can zoom into their other bodies, and acquire Anunnaki's supernatural faculties.
- I have used the words supernatural faculties instead of supernatural powers, because the enlightened and initiated ones are peaceful, and do not use physical power, brutal force or any aggressive means to reach their objectives.
- The use of violence against humans and animals, even aggressive thoughts and harmful intentions annihilate all chances to acquire Anunnaki's extraordinary faculties.
- Your Double can easily read your thoughts.
- If your thoughts are malicious, your Double will prevent you from zooming yourself into its ethereal molecules. Therefore, you have to control your temper, remain calm, and show serenity in your thoughts, intentions and actions.

- You Double is very delicate, even though it can accomplish the toughest missions and penetrate the thickest barriers. Any indication of violence or ill intention triggers a pulse that blocks your passage to the ethereal sphere of your Double.
- Once you enter your Double, you will be able to use it in so many beautiful and effective ways as:
  1- A protective shield against danger,
  2- An effective apparatus to protect yourself in hostile and dangerous situations,
  3- A tool to develop your abilities to learn many languages, and enhance your artistic creativity,
  4- A stimulus to increase the capacity of your memory,
  5- Instrument to heal wounds and internal injuries. No, you will not become a surgeon, but you will be able to stop internal bleeding, and eliminate pain,
  6- A vehicle to visit distant places and even enter restricted areas for good causes. In brief, the possibilities are endless.
- Once you are in a perfect harmony with your Double, and your physical organism is elevated to a higher vibrational level through your union with your Double, you will be able to walk through solid substances such as walls, sheets of glasses and metal.
- You become effective in controlling metal and de-fragmenting molecules of any substance. This will allow you to transmute, change and alter the properties of any object known to mankind.
- But if you use these supernatural faculties to hurt others, or for personal and selfish gain, you will loose them for good, and you will be accountable for such malicious use in the other dimension. And this could delay your entrance through the Ba'ab.

*** *** ***

During one of the readings, I saw with my own eyes, the honorable Ulema Albakri dematerializing and walking through a wall. Many of the students, including myself thought it was an illusion, a trick performed by the teacher. We became suspicious. We were wrong, because when we began to search for him inside the room, and check the thickness of the wall, we heard him calling us from outside the room. He was standing under a pomegranate tree in the garden. And in a blink of an eye, he materialized inside the room, as if he has never left us. We became speechless.

One student asked him: How long it would take me to do this? Can I do what you did? And the honorable Ulema replied: "Only if you free your mind, and clean your thoughts.

To cross over to the other side, you need to establish a direct rapport with your Double, and invite others to your heart..."

*** *** ***

Contacting the Dead through your Double

The following is taken from a Kira'a by an Ulema, dialogues with students, and an honorable teacher's answers to questions by novices.

Question:

A novice asked the teacher these questions: Can we contact our departed parents through our double? And is it dangerous to contact the dead?

The Theosophy view:

Before I give you the answer of the Ulema, I would like to share with you the interesting view of Theosophy on the subject, in case you are not familiar with.

Millions of Americans strongly believe in its dogma, and explanation of the mental-spiritual contact between a living person and a dead person.

Although it differs from the Ulema's concept because it focuses heavily on the notion of Kama, its metaphoric depiction coincides to a certain degree with the Ulema's vision.

85

According to the Secret Doctrine of Theosophy, many people feel that mediums (Enlightened for the Ulema) could bring them in contact with the "Spirit" (Mind for the Ulema) of their dear departed ones.

The Theosophy teaches that what one comes across is only the kama-rupic shell of the dead. (Memory projection for the Ulema) It is the psychic corpse of the deceased person, which gives off impressions like a gramophone record.

This activity is dangerous to both sitters and mediums of the séance room.

A medium makes connection with the kama-rupic shell with the aid of his nervous fluid and also the elementals.

There is, besides, the presence of "elementaries" or depraved souls at almost all séances. (For the Ulema, souls are never present during any contact.) (Sources: The Ocean of Theosophy; The Book of Rama-Dosh.)

Always according to Theosophy: There are numerous difficulties and dangers.

There are several layers of astral (Dimensions or frequencies of the Double for the Ulema) light and only a true clairvoyant (Enlightened for the Ulema) can look into all the layers. There are delusions.

An untrained clairvoyant (Initiated for the Ulema) is deluded, as he/she is not able to differentiate between the picture he/she sees of an idea or thought in a person's mind, and the picture of an actual event. For example, a mother who is anxious about her child may merely imagine that child meeting with an accident and thus form a picture. An untrained person will see this picture (Which is solely due to emotion and imagination on the part of the mother) and predict an accident. Then again there is reversion of images.

The figure 6 would be seen as 9, and 9 as 6, etc. Sometimes a picture could be colored by one's own emotions and thoughts. Most of these are psychic visions (Mental projection for the Ulema.) (Sources: M. Judge's "Shall We Teach Clairvoyance?" H. P. Blavatsky; Teosophia; Book of Rama-Dosh.)

Excerpts from the honorable Ulema's answer to the question: Can we contact our departed parents through our double?
And is it dangerous to contact the dead?

- No such contact is possible. However, few enlightened ones have succeeded in contacting the Mind of the deceased ONLY during the first 40 days of the departure of the dead.
- During the 40 days period, a contact could occur, if the deceased have not yet entered his Double.
- Once the deceased has entered his Double, it becomes very difficult to sense the frequencies of the Mind. It is very difficult but not impossible, especially if the deceased has a noble Mind, and that Mind either initiated a contact or was still on the perimeters of the physical and non physical dimensions.
- Once the Mind enters the Fifth dimension, contacting the dead becomes an impossibility.
- The Anunnaki-Ulema are capable of contacting other Minds and non-physical entities in other dimensions, multiple universes, and parallel dimensions through the Miraya (Anunnaki cosmic monitor, also called mirror.)
- A Double can contact another Double in the after-life, even if both of them live in different dimensions.
- Sometimes, your Double tries to contact you while you are still alive. And because you are still alive on Earth, and your Double exists in a non-physical dimension, the contact occurs in many ways, forms and means. Poets call this contact inspiration. Psychics call it channeling. Spiritists call it communication with the dead. The truth is this:

A-No psychic, no spiritist, no living creature on this Earth can communicate with the dead.
B-You cannot command your Double to appear before you. Only the enlightened ones can.

C-Your Double can initiate a contact through telepathy, projection of thoughts, and ethereal apparition on smooth surfaces like mirror, glass, and limpid waters.

D-The Anunnaki can compose and de-compose the molecules and cells of the human body, and alter the first elements of your creation (In other words: DNA). This, allows them to project, materialize, teleport and duplicate so many Doubles, including yours.

E-When the Anunnaki created you, they have also created an original copy of yourself and stored it in their archives. This copy was stored and recorded as your blueprint.

F- The Anunnaki can project your blueprint on a holographic screen right before your eyes.

G-This projection allows you to see and read your past, present and future life illustrated in sequences.

H-Attempt to contact your Double could be harmful, if you are not initiated.

It could cause:

(a) mental perturbation;
(b) psychological confusion;
(c) psychosomatic disequilibrium.

*** *** ***

Question:
A novice asked the teacher this question:
What do we get from zooming into our Double?

Learning how to communicate with your Double

Talking to my teacher...

Long, longtime ago, during my first year of apprenticeship, I asked my teacher if it was possible to meet with my Double face to face, and ask for some reasonable favors, or perhaps help...and the Honorable teacher interrupted me and said– always genuinely smiling - : "First of all, my dear son, you do not contact your Double to ask for favors.

You have to remember, that selfishness is self-destructive. Instead of asking for favors, you should seek knowledge first." He paused for a few seconds, gazing at me, as if he was reading my mind - probably he was - and continued: "Your Double knows exactly what you need...and when in you are in need, your Double will come to you." I was strucked by his answer because other Ulema used to tell us that nobody can call his Double unless he is one of the enlightened ones.

But short after, he explained to me that the Nizam is merciful and just. He said: "The initiated are privileged, but also those who are pure in heart can communicate with their Double without going through the initiation ceremonies.

The major difference between the initiated and non-initiated is, that the communication with the Double is much easier for the initiated because they know the process and techniques, while the non-initiated have to rely solely on a very deep introspection which is not easy at all, and quite often, it can be very disorienting...

I will give you an example so you would understand. Initiated and non-initiated are like passengers on a ship. Some travel first class, some second class, and others travel third class. All are on the same ship. Those who travel first class are allowed to visit the decks and facilities of the second class.

Those who travel second class can walk around the decks of the third class.

But those who travel third class are restricted to their third class area, they are not allowed to go up to the second or third class.

Now, you are taking the train, can you with your second class ticket sleep in a first class compartment?

You can't unless you upgrade your ticket.

The initiated like the first class passengers have certain privileges. On a ship or a train, it is a matter of buying a more expensive ticket.

For the initiated is not a ticket but spiritual merits. These are the privileges I am talking about..."

I continued: "There are so many good people in the world who live far away, and for so many reasons cannot come to the Ulema to study and receive initiation.

89

Do you think it would be fair to deprive them from those privileges, simply because they did not study with you. How about their good deeds and merits?

How do you explain this to me? Somebody might be a very good person, but he is very sick, even paralyzed, and cannot come all the way to Cairo to study with us...don't you think this person deserves a break?"

The honorable master replied: "Of course he does, this is why he has to practice. It is not going to be easy because he will be not receiving guidance and orientation from the honorable teachers, but he might succeed in communicating with his Double for a very short time...To tell you the truth my son, many have received sudden enlightenment without studying the books, and never knew how it did happen...it is not the teacher who decides who should be enlightened and who deserves to obtain knowledge from his Double. It is not the teacher, but one's good merits, and honorable deeds..."

*** *** ***

Chapter 5
Reincarnation

- There is no reincarnation of bodies or souls on Earth.
- Reincarnation in the after-life.
- The Fifth dimension.
- The honorable Ulema said.
- The after-life is a wonderful place where we reach the state of quasi-perfection.
- The quasi-perfection manifests itself in.
- The collective Mind's transmigration phenomenon
- The Mind's reincarnation in the after-life.

*** *** ***

Chapter 5
Reincarnation
There is no reincarnation of bodies or souls on Earth.

The Anunnaki taught the Ulema, that there is no reincarnation of bodies or souls on Earth, but in other dimensions, a process of purification and learning in the form of Mind transmigration occurs and re-occurs indefinitely.

The honorable Ulema's comments on the subject of reincarnations are:

- When the Anunnaki created us on this Earth, they mixed in a mold, an earthly element called "Turab" with part of their essence (DNA).

Note:

a-**Mold** means container, an incubator or a similar tool.

b-**Turab** means dirt, sands, carbon, fossils, etc...It is not necessarily clay as we know it today, and as it was alleged or explained by other authors. Some enlightened teachers have said, that Turab or the clay mentioned in the Sumerian texts could also be sea shells. This was mentioned in ancient Phoenicians texts, epics and terracotta.

c-**Part of their essence** means DNA or an extract from their genes that were not contaminated on Earth.

- Because the mix did not contain what humans call "Soul", the soul never entered our bodies. There is another non-physical element called Mind that substitutes for the soul. (Buddhism shares this concept.)
- The Mind does not reincarnate on Earth. No reason to.
- The Mind evolves in our lives according to the Anunnaki's blueprint, and in virtue of a constant learning on Earth. This is one of the biggest differences between the Anunnaki-Ulema's Mind and humans' concept of soul.

93

- The Mind (Soul to others) does not evolve or acquire more knowledge and wisdom by returning to Earth, and reincarnating in other human bodies, because neither the human body, nor Earth's teachings surpass the level and standards of the teachings of the Anunnaki, and the amount of knowledge to be gained in higher dimensions. Thus, your Mind (Soul) should go somewhere else to acquire more elevated knowledge and purify itself. The corrupt and contaminated environment of Earth and human beings' societies do not allow the Mind (Soul) to reach a higher level of enlightenment. Earth is the lowest habitat in the universe. And humans are the lowest living thinking creatures in the universe. Returning to Earth as a reincarnated soul will defeat all purposes.
- Instead, the Mind (Soul) searches for a purified level of existence, increases its mental (Spiritual to others) qualities, and evolves where the ultimate purification and intelligence (Spirituality to others) exist. Earth is not such a place! And humans are not those pure and ultimately developed beings to help your soul to reach perfection and ultimate goodness.
- There is no logic to the idea of the reincarnation of the soul and its return to Earth. You have been here before, and you have seen how people treat people. You heard so many contradicting ideas and teachings about the truth, the human salvation, the true prophets, the elaborate speeches of your preachers and teachers, and so on. You heard them once, twice, and zillion of times...it is more than enough. If you return again to Earth, you will hear over and over again the same old stories. Perhaps new streets were paved, and new names given to new companies, and new car are designed, but do all these things help your soul? Don't you think if your soul goes somewhere else, where there are no greed, no wars, no killings, no violence, no hatred, no fanaticism, no racism, no mistreating animals, and no betrayal...it would be far better and more beneficial to your soul?

94

- Why Jesus, Mohammad, Moses, Einstein, and the prophets of God did not return to Earth? This, you will figure it out on your own!

*** *** ***

Reincarnation in the after-life.

The Anunnaki-Ulema said, that the Mind (Soul to others) is not stagnant. It evolves, and continues to evolve and progress for hundreds of thousands of years after death on Earth, - the deterioration of the physical body, that is.
But in order to evolve, the Mind (Soul) must reach a higher sphere of knowledge and goodness. And that sphere begins with the Fifth dimension.

*** *** ***

The Fifth dimension:
The honorable Ulema said:

- The Fifth dimension is just the beginning, because there are seven dimensions.
- Six dimensions constitute the world of the after-life for humans. (Only four are known to us.)
- The Seventh dimension is reserved to the "Khalek" (Creator of the human race).
- No human (Mind or soul of humans) can reach and enter the Seventh dimension.
- I mentioned seven dimensions only, because these are the world beyond for the humans.
- We start on Earth, because we were created by the Anunnaki on Earth. And from Earth, we go higher.
- And higher means the other six dimensions.

- The world of humans (Physical and non-physical) is made out of these dimensions that constitute the beginning, the end and the entire human world.
- Other living entities on other planets and stars have different universes, different places for their after-life and the world beyond.
- They evolve differently.
- They have different Khalek (Different Creator, or different God).
- For each universe, there is a different Khalek. The Greek philosophers and sages of ancient civilizations on Earth were not stupid. They mentioned it in their writings and secret doctrines, but they did not figure it right. In the Anunnaki's metaphysics, there are no pagan gods, but a continuum of intelligence and creation. A sort of "All that Is".
- Humans do not reincarnate in the after-life.
- Humans through their Mind (Soul to others) move from one dimension to another dimension, and this could take hundreds of thousands of years.
- First, humans (Mind of the humans) must reach the perfect state of purification.
- Next, humans (Mind of Humans) must acquire the "Soudk" (The ultimate knowledge and truth). This is usually acquired in the Fifth dimension, not in the Fourth dimension.
- In the Fifth dimension, humans who are no longer humans but divine beings, retain many of the earthly properties they acquired on Earth (The Good ones), and receive extraordinary faculties and capabilities, such as:

*** *** ***

The after-life is a wonderful place where we reach the state of quasi-perfection.

The quasi-perfection manifests itself in:

- a-Bending time
- b-Bending space,
- c-Mental teleportation to the entire six dimensions,
- d-Reversing Spatial Memory,
- e-Creating new living creatures,
- f-Taking part in the creation of new universes;
- g-Shifting space's frontiers;
- h-Superposing parallel dimensions;
- i-Inhabiting simultaneously multiple universes;
- j-Identifying all the Ba'abs and Madkals,
- k-Influencing destinies;
- l-Creating entities' blueprints;
- m-Accelerating time;
- n-Reversing time;
- o-Halting time and distances' dilatation,
- p-And of course interacting with living creatures in all the dimensions and Earth as well.

This is how the purified Mind (Soul to others), evolves, transmigrates and reincarnates in the world beyond.
Reincarnation in the after-life is simply acquiring extraordinary knowledge and faculties, always according to the blueprint and ever-evolving nature of humans as created by the Anunnaki.

*** *** ***

97

The collective Mind's transmigration phenomenon.
The Mind's reincarnation in the after-life.

Another fascinating aspect of the Mind's reincarnation in the after-life is the collective Mind's transmigration phenomenon, where all Minds through the Conduit tap into the cosmic depot of ultimate knowledge; an infinite registry of supernatural powers and a cosmic library of all what there is in the universe. (Akashic Records to others.)

Fortunately to humans, they can benefit enormously from the pure Minds (Souls, Spirits of the departed loved ones, to others) and the positive energies of the after life's dimensions though guided contacts.

We are not alone on Earth, in the universe, and in the after-life.

There are noble entities who are watching over us, some are unreachable, others are so close to us. There is hope for all of us, only if we try to free ourselves from greed, hatred, envy and violence.

One way to start is to talk to our Double.

If this notion is hard to swallow, never mind, call your Double CONSCIENCE if this makes you feel better.

*** *** ***

Chapter 6

The Frontiers of the World Beyond The Anunnaki's Physical and Non-Physical Dimensions

- Frontiers of the world beyond: The Anunnaki's physical and non-physical dimensions.
- Do we live in dimensions according to what the Anunnaki have created?
- How many dimensions are related to us and to the Anunnaki?
- And where do these dimensions and the world of the Anunnaki start?
- Answer of the honorable Ulema.
- As far as humans are concerned, there are two Anunnaki's worlds: "Sama" and "Falak".
- 1-The first world is the Sama.
- 2-The second world is the "Falak", or "Dounia".
- Do we live in dimensions according to what the Anunnaki have created?
- Does this mean that the Fourth dimension is the world beyond?
- Would it be safe to say that we live in two dimensions in the same time?"

*** *** ***

99

Chapter 6
Frontiers of the World Beyond: The Anunnaki's Physical and Non-Physical Dimensions

The following is taken from a Kira'a (Reading) by an Ulema, dialogues with students, and an honorable teacher's answers to questions by novices.

*** *** ***

Questions:
A student asked the teacher the following:
Do we live in dimensions according to what the Anunnaki have created?
How many dimensions are related to us and to the Anunnaki?
And where do these dimensions and the world of the Anunnaki start?

Answer of the honorable Ulema:
As far as humans are concerned, there are two Anunnaki's worlds: "Sama" and "Falak".

1-The first world is the Sama:

- It exists while humans are still alive on planet earth.
- Sama is the extraterrestrial world, where the Anunnaki and other extraterrestrial races live.
- Sama existed in the universe billions of years before planet earth and the human race were created.
- Sama is a physical world. Its atmospheric properties vary from one planet to another planet, and from one star to another star.

101

- For instance, Ashtari (Nibiru to others) has quasi-similar Earth's atmosphere, however the air is denser, the climate is heavier, the days are longer, and it has four celestial objects orbiting it.
- Although humans could live on Ashtari (Nibiru), certain surgical operations are needed to allow the human body to adapt to the new atmospheric conditions and environment on Ashtari (Nibiru).
- So, the physical world of the Anunnaki would allow humans to continue to live outside planet earth, and inhabit Ashtari.
- You could call Sama the bodily world of humans. Because they can travel to Sama and live on Sama as physical creatures.
- Sometimes we refer to Sama as "Maddi", meaning the physical dimension outside planet earth. And Maddi has living conditions almost similar to those on planet earth. Maddi has weather, trees, lakes, plains, mountains, cities, streets, etc.
- In other words, the Sama is the world of the living human beings, and extraterrestrials.
- It starts outside our solar system; billions of light years separate planet earth from Sama.
- Bashar (Humans) have not reached Sama yet. But extraterrestrials have reached planet earth some 500,000 years ago (More or less).
- Some extraterrestrial races are still on planet earth, and have offspring and descendants living among us.

Author's note: I have described in detail Sama (Maddi) and the living conditions of the Anunnaki on Nibiru in my book "What Extraterrestrials and Anunnaki Want You to Know", published in 2008. In the book "Anunnaki Ultimatum: End of Time", that I have co-authored with Ilil Arbel, I provided ample description and analyses of the social daily life of the Anunnaki on Nibiru, their social classes, occupation, families, technology, inventions, etc...

2-The second world is the "Falak", or "Dounia":

- Falak (Dounia) is not a physical world.
- No living human beings as physical creatures live in this second world.
- You have to remember that physical objects including human beings cannot enter a non-physical world. Thus, Falak (Dounia) is not a world where human beings could live with their physical bodies.
- Falak (Dounia) is the world of the human mind.
- The human mind was created by the Anunnaki.
- The human mind can manifest itself as the Double of a physical body.
- Falak (Dounia) consists of seven different "Woujoud", meaning existences.
- Three of these Woujoud already exist in a physical-nonphysical sphere of illusion, called "Kha-Da'h". Planet earth is one of these three existences. But these three existences do not count as meaningful dimensions. This is why we start counting with the Fourth dimension as the first sphere of Falak (Dounia).
- The first Woujoud is known to us as the Fourth dimension, and it is called "Nafis-Ra".
- The second Woujoud is known to us as the Fifth dimension, and it is called "Fik'r-Ra".
- The third Woujoud is known to us as the Sixth dimension, and it is called "Kadosh-Ra" or "Koudous-Ra".
- The fourth Woujoud is known to us as the Seventh dimension, and it is called "Khalek-Ra".
- In other words, the Falak (Dounia) is the world of human beings who continue to live through their mind. Extraterrestrials of a very high vibrational state could share this sphere with the purified mind of humans (The deceased ones).

103

- Falak (Dounia) starts as soon as we die. It is neither outside nor inside our solar system, and no light years separate humans from any dimension or state of existence in Falak (Dounia)
- Some Bashar (Humans) have already reached different vibrational levels and spheres in Falak (Dounia).

*** *** ***

Do we live in dimensions according to what the Anunnaki have created?

This is one of the most frequently asked questions by novices and students. Generally, the Ulema are not concerned with issues of a metaphysical nature, because they do not believe that the physical world is completely separated from the non-physical world.

They do not see the universe the way we do.

Therefore, everything is part of something else. One Ulema once said, talking to a student: "Even this rock and this tree leaf are part of you. We are made of the same material." This could be interpreted metaphorically, but there is a deep scientific veracity attached to it.

The honorable Ulema continued: "Yes, a rock is a rock. It is physical. It is real. You can touch it and you can weight it.

But that's not all...it is not all of it, because it has an additional dimension you can't see with your eyes. It does not start and end where you start to touch it, and where you finish touching it.

Once, your "Rou'ya" (Third Eye to others) opens up, you begin to see a larger size of the rock, and discover its hidden properties...this is why we call earth, the life we live, our desires and our ambitions ILLUSION."

104

The honorable Ulema continues: "Yes we do live in physical and non-physical dimensions according to what the Anunnaki have created..."

Author's note: I will mention herewith parts of his answers that are related to the question:

- The Anunnaki have created us on earth to serve their needs. Their intentions were to create a race that could carry heavy physical load and do intense physical labor. This was the initial and prime objective.
- Thus, the "Naphsiya" (DNA) they put in us had limited lifespan, and mental faculties.
- Later on, they discovered that they had to prolong the human lifespan and add more developed mental faculties, so they added the "Hara-Kiya" (Internal energy or physical strength).
- Few generations later, the early human beings stock evolves considerably, because the Anunnaki added fully operational Mind in the human body.
- To do so, they installed a Conduit with limited capabilities.
- In the same time, this Conduit was also installed into the prototype of the human body. Thus, through the Mind, the physical body of the humans got linked to the Double.
- This non-physical link created a Fourth dimension for all of us. In fact, it did not create a Fourth dimension per se, rather it activated it.
- So now, at that stage, humans had a physical dimension (Life on earth), and not-a-totally separated non-physical dimension called "Nafis-Ra".
- So, yes, Bashar (Humans) became destined to acquire two dimensions, as exactly the Anunnaki decided.
- Later on, centuries upon centuries, the human mind began to evolve, because the other Mind, call it now the Double or prototype began to evolve simultaneously and in sync.

- The more the prototype is advanced the more "Physical Mind" becomes alert, creative and multidimensional.
- But we are not trapped, and our mind is no longer conditioned by the Anunnaki.
- The Anunnaki gave us all the choices, opportunities, freewill and freedom to learn on our own and progress. This is why we are accountable and responsible for everything we do and think about.
- Because of the evolution of our mind, and realization of an inner knowledge of our surroundings, and understanding what is right and what is wrong, a major mental faculty emerged in all of us: Conscience.

*** *** ***

More questions:
Does this mean that the Fourth dimension is the world beyond?
The honorable Ulema answered: "The Fourth Dimension is just the beginning of the world beyond. As we progress in the after-life, we discover new dimensions and new forms of life.

Would it be safe to say that we live in two dimensions in the same time?"
The honorable Ulema replied: "Very wise...very wise indeed, my dear Kumar...yes, we do live simultaneously in two dimensions. One, we are aware of, we sense it and we see it, the other, we could reach it and understand it through:
- 1-Our mind,
- 2-Communicating with our Double,
- 3-Mental introspection,
- 4-A pure diet,
- 5-Projection of thoughts,
- 6-A physical-mental retreat that opens our Conduit.

106

Chapter 7
The Conduit

- Ulema: The Conduit links us to the entire knowledge of the universe.
- I. Introduction.
- II. Developing the Conduit.
- III. Haridu "Haridu-ilmu".
- IV. Jaba.
- V. Interpretation of messages sent to the Conduit "Haridu", "Haridu-ilmu".
- 1. Definition
- 2. Ulema Rabbi Mordechai explains Haridu–Conduit Equation.
- VI. Fik'r "Fik-R'r", "Fik.Ra.Sa".
- Metaphysical-religious context.
- VII. Fikrama "Fikr-Rama".
- VIII. Kira-Fik.

*** *** ***

Chapter 7
The Conduit
Ulema: The Conduit links us to the entire knowledge of the universe

I. Introduction:
The Ulema teach that the Conduit links us to the Anunnaki's Miraya that contains, stores and reflects all the knowledge, sounds, ideas, events, thoughts, past, present and future that exist in the universe. However, they do agree with the notion of the holographic screen.

In fact, the Ulema were the first to talk and teach about spatial holography, holography screen, and Collective Mind, sometimes called the "Anunnaki Collective Depot of Knowledge" shared by all the Anunnaki communities' members.

The Ulema teach that human life is neither a restricted part of the divine creation, nor the creation itself. Thus, it is not limited by time, space, and the frontiers of a divine matrix.

*** *** ***

II. Developing the Conduit:
There are techniques which are partially physical and partially mental. You could refer to them as psychosomatic. As a beginner, even though your Conduit is now open, you cannot tap directly into it, because consciously, you don't even know where it is located in your brain. By adopting some postures and positions, you will send sensations to your brain.

These positions will create internal muscular vibrations, and your mind will read them. You will be sending mental visionary lines, and these will activate the cell which is responsible for imagination.

By the power of concentration and introspection, you will start to get intensified activity in the brain. This causes a buzz vibration in the brain the Conduit begins to detect.

109

Then, the Conduit will absorb the vibrations and organize them, and from that moment on, the Conduit will take over.

To summarize, by attempting certain activities, you are sending a message to your Conduit. It will take some time, because at the beginning, your Conduit may not catch the messages, or if it does catch them, may not interpret the messages correctly, because the Conduit is not one hundred percent awake.
With practice, the Conduit becomes familiar with these type of messages, and it begins to give them codes.
Each activity would have its own code.
One thing must be understood. You cannot do these techniques to amuse yourself, since they simply will not work unless there is a purpose to the activity, and it must be a beneficial, positive purpose.

*** *** ***

III. Haridu "Haridu-ilmu":
Interpretation of messages sent to the Conduit in an Anunnaki's or a human's brain cell. Also, it applies to missing or misinterpreting a message by the Conduit.

On this, Ulema Rabbi Mordechai said verbatim:
- "First of all, you have to remember that your mind (Your brain) has nothing to do with your Conduit. Even though, your brain is functioning wonderfully and you are doing great things in your life, not all the cells in your brain have been used.
- There are so many regions in our brain that have not been explored yet by science.
- In those many unexplored regions of the brain, are so many cells yet to be discovered, located and localized. And above all, we need to learn how they function.
- In that mysterious undiscovered region of the brain, the Conduit exists. It could be in the right or left side of your brain, or just adjacent to line dividing the two parts.

110

- In the Conduit, there are so many cells, each one with a very defined and particular extraordinary faculty/power, that needs to be activated.
- For instance, one cell triggers the faculty of reading others' thoughts, another cell (Or cells) is responsible for the faculty of teleportation, so on.
- If those cells are not activated, you will not be able to do all those wonderful things.
- So, you have to consider the Conduit as a bank where so many cells are deposited. And there are hundreds of thousands of cells deposited in the Conduit.
- Each cell has a precise function and an invisible location.
- This means that the Conduit can do so many things, if cells are activated. It would be impossible in one lifespan to develop and activate all the cells.
- Three or four fully activated cells is more than enough. With four activated cells you can do four great miracles by earth's standards.
- But for the cell to produce this extraordinary power, the cell must be able first to understand what you want to do.
- For instance, you cannot tell or command your cell "go ahead and make me fly or let me learn a new language in one hour."
- You should first learn how to send your command to your cell. There is a technique for this.
- Your Ulema teacher knows how to put you on the right track.
- Let's assume you have sent a message (A thought, a wish) to your cell. What's next?
- Well, the message enters your Conduit. Your conduit acting as a supervisor, and as the main receiver reads your message and directs your message to the appropriate cell.
- Your Conduit knows which cell is activated and designed to comply with your request.

111

- Instantly, the cell receives the Conduit transfer (Meaning your message.)
- Then what? The cell reads your message.
- If your message was sent correctly, then the cell will accept it and give it a code. So, if in the future you ask again your Conduit to do the same thing you have asked in the past, the cell will execute your request in a fraction of a second.
- In other words, each request is coded, and stored in your cell.
- Only coded messages are stored in your Conduit.
- How would you know if you have or have not sent a message correctly to your Conduit? You will know right away. It is very simple. If you have not been trained, you wouldn't know where and how to start in the first place.
- This is the reason why your Conduit did not catch your message(s).
- You asked "Does this mean that my Conduit is not receiving clear messages from me? And the answer is yes! Your Conduit received something, a thought, a feeling, a wish, a request, call it whatever you want, but your message was not clear to your Conduit, because you did not send your message according to the rules.
- What are these rules?
- They are explained below. But continue to read this first.
- And then you asked: "And how can I send clear messages my Conduit can catch and understand?
- You have to use the "Transmission of Mind" technique. Practice this technique before you send messages to your Conduit. For example, in the past, the SOS (Morse Code) was used by ships, planes, military troops and others.
- The person who has sent the message (Morse) knew the Code; he/she knew how to tap it.
- Each word had a code...one dot, two dots, three dots, one dash, two dashes, three dashes, one dit, two dits, one space, two spaces, three spaces, etc.

- There is a sequence of pulses and marks. And the person who received the message knew how what these dots, and dashes meant.
- This is how and why he/she was able to read the message or decipher it, if it was a secret message.
- Your Conduit works exactly in the same way.
- Your Ulema teacher will tell you exactly what dots and sequences to use.
- If your Conduit is hundred percent awake, meaning Open (After training completion), the Conduit will immediately interpret/translate and understand your dots, dashes and sequences.
- Consider those dashes and dots a "Password", a log-in information, a key to open the contact with your Conduit, just like the password you use to open your computer or have access to some websites.
- In the Book of Ramadosh, you will find several passages referring to the brain waves and mind frequencies, and some techniques used to direct thoughts and mind energies.
- Your Conduit has its own mode. As long as your Conduit is not activated, it remains free of your control. Once your Conduit is activated, you become the stimulus and the manager of your Conduit.
- The Conduit works partially when it is not activated.
- And partially means reacting by not acting.
- The Conduit functions all the time regardless of your state of awareness, enlightenment or readiness. But it will not give you data and information.
- Everything the Conduit finds is instantly deposited in its compound.
- You will not find what's in there, until the Conduit is fully activated.
- Consider it for now as a depot of knowledge; a sort of a personal bank account where your daily balance is constantly increasing, however, you are not allowed to have access to your bank account.

113

- So, nothing is lost.
- Your Conduit collects and stores information all the time, and from various sources, times, and spheres.

*** *** ***

IV. Jaba:
In Ana'kh, the word Jaba means many things. For example:
- **a**-The "Net Jaba" is a time-space pocket.
- **b**-The "Jaba-Garidu" is related to the "Conduit" cell, and adjacent cells in the brain.
- **c**-The "Jaba-Abru" is related to time management, using the power of mind to achieve multiple and lengthy tasks simultaneously.

Note: Please refer to the book "The Book of Ramadosh", latest edition, 2010, where you will find an in-depth study of the subject.

*** *** ***

V. Interpretation of messages sent to the Conduit "Haridu", "Haridu-ilmu":
1. Definition
II. Ulema Rabbi Mordechai explains Haridu-Conduit Equation

---

1. Definition:
Interpretation of messages sent to the "Conduit" in an Anunnaki's or a human's brain cell. Also, it applies to missing or misinterpreting a message by the Conduit.

*** *** ***

2. Mordechai explains Haridu–Conduit Equation:

114

Ulema Mordechai said verbatim:
- "First of all, you have to remember that your mind (Your brain) has nothing to do with your Conduit. Even though, your brain is functioning wonderfully and you are doing great things in your life, not all the cells in your brain have been used.
- There are so many regions in our brain that have not been explored yet by science.
- In those many unexplored regions of the brain, are so many cells yet to be discovered, located and localized. And above all, we need to learn how they function.
- In that mysterious undiscovered region of the brain, the Conduit exists. It could be in the right or left side of your brain, or just adjacent to line dividing the two parts.
- In the Conduit, there are so many cells, each one with a very defined and particular extraordinary faculty/power, that needs to be activated.
- For instance, one cell triggers the faculty of reading others' thoughts, another cell (Or cells) is responsible for the faculty of teleportation, so on.
- If those cells are not activated, you will not be able to do all those wonderful things.
- So, you have to consider the Conduit as a bank where so many cells are deposited.
- And there are hundreds of thousands of cells deposited in the Conduit.
- Each cell has a precise function and an invisible location.
- This means that the Conduit can do so many things, if cells are activated. It would be impossible in one lifespan to develop and activate all the cells.
- Three or four fully activated cells is more than enough. With four activated cells you can do four great miracles by earth's standards.
- But for the cell to produce this extraordinary power, the cell must be able first to understand what you want to do.

115

- For instance, you cannot tell or command your cell "go ahead and make me fly or let me learn a new language in one hour."
- You should first learn how to send your command to your cell. There is a technique for this.
- Your Ulema teacher knows how to put you on the right track.
- Let's assume you have sent a message (A thought, a wish) to your cell. What's next? Well, the message enters your Conduit. Your conduit acting as a supervisor, and as the main receiver reads your message and directs your message to the appropriate cell.
- Your Conduit knows which cell is activated and designed to comply with your request.
- Instantly, the cell receives the Conduit transfer (Meaning your message.)
- Then what? The cell reads your message.
- If your message was sent correctly, then the cell will accept it and give it a code. So, if in the future you ask again your Conduit to do the same thing you have asked in the past, the cell will execute your request in a fraction of a second.
- In other words, each request is coded, and stored in your cell.
- Only coded messages are stored in your Conduit.
- How would you know if you have or have not sent a message correctly to your Conduit? You will know right away. It is very simple. If you have not been trained, you wouldn't know where and how to start in the first place.
- This is the reason why your Conduit did not catch your message(s).
- You asked "Does this mean that my Conduit is not receiving clear messages from me? And the answer is yes! Your Conduit received something, a thought, a feeling, a wish, a request, call it whatever you want, but your message was not clear to your Conduit, because you did not send your message according to the rules.

116

- What are these rules?
- They are explained below. But continue to read this first.
- And then you asked: "And how can I send clear messages my Conduit can catch and understand?
- You have to use the "Transmission of Mind" technique. Practice this technique before you send messages to your Conduit. For example, in the past, the SOS (Morse Code) was used by ships, planes, military troops and others. The person who has sent the message (Morse) knew the Code; he/she knew how to tap it.
- Each word had a code...one dot, two dots, three dots, one dash, two dashes, three dashes, one dit, two dits, one space, two spaces, three spaces, etc.
- There is a sequence of pulses and marks.
- And the person who received the message knew how what these dots, and dashes meant.
- This is how and why he/she was able to read the message or decipher it, if it was a secret message.
- Your Conduit works exactly in the same way.
- Your Ulema teacher will tell you exactly what dots and sequences to use.
- If your Conduit is hundred percent awake, meaning open (After training completion), the Conduit will immediately interpret and translate and understand your dots, dashes and sequences.
- Consider those dashes and dots a "Password", a logging-in information, a key to open the contact with your Conduit, just like the password you use to open your computer or have access to some websites.
- In the Book of Ramadosh, you will find several passages referring to the brain waves and mind frequencies, and some techniques used to direct thoughts and mind energies.
- Your Conduit has its own mode.
- As long as your Conduit is not activated, it remains free of your control.

- Once your Conduit is activated, you become the stimulus and the manager of your Conduit.
- The Conduit works partially when it is not activated.
- And partially means reacting by not acting.
- The Conduit functions all the time regardless of your state of awareness, enlightenment or readiness.
- But it will not give you data and information.
- Everything the Conduit finds or retrieves is always instantly deposited/stored in its compound., but not yet interpreted or understood, until the Conduit is activated or open.
- You will not find what's in there, until the Conduit is fully activated.
- Consider it for now as a depot of knowledge; a sort of a personal bank account where your daily balance is constantly increasing, however, you are not allowed to have access to your bank account.
- So, nothing is lost.
- Your Conduit collects and stores information all the time, and from various sources, times, and spheres.

*** *** ***

VI. Fik'r "Fik-R'r", "Fik.Ra.Sa":
The ability of reading others' thoughts.
The esoteric Arabic word "Firasa" is derived from Fik.Ra.Sa. It means in Arabic the ability to read thoughts, to understand the psyche of a person just by looking at him/her.
The Ulema used Fik'r to read the mind, learn about the intentions of others, and assess the level of intelligence of people.
The soul is an invention of early humans who needed to believe in a next life.
It was through the soul that mortals could and would hope to continue to live after death.
Soul as an element or a substance does not exist anywhere inside the human body.

118

Instead, there is a non-physical substance called "Fik'r" that makes the brain function, and it is the brain that keeps the body working, not the soul.

The "Fik'r" was the primordial element used by the Anunnaki at the time they created the final form of the human race. Fik'r was not used in the early seven prototypes of the creation of mankind according to the Sumerian texts.

The "Fik'r", although it is the primordial source of life for our physical body, it is not to be considered as DNA, because DNA is a part of "Fik'r"; DNA is the physical description of our genes, a sort of a series of formulas, numbers and sequences of what there in our body, the data and history of our genes, genetic origin, ethnicity, race, so on. Thus Fik'r includes DNA.

Ulema said: "Consider Fik'r as a cosmic-sub-atomic-intellectual-extraterrestrial (Meaning non-physical, non-earthly) depot of all what it constituted, constitutes and shall continue to constitute everything about you. And it is infinitesimally small.

However, it can expand to an imaginable dimension, size and proportions. It stays alive and continues to grow after we pass away if it is still linked to the origin of its creation, in our case the Anunnaki.

The Fik'r is linked to the Anunnaki our creators through a "Conduit" found in the cells of the brain.

For now, consider Fik'r as a small molecule, a bubble. After death, this bubble leaves the body. In fact, the body dies as soon as the bubble leaves the body.

The body dies because the bubble leaves the body. Immediately, with one tenth of one million of a second, the molecule or the bubble frees itself from any and everything physical, including the atmosphere, the air, and the light; absolutely everything we can measure, and everything related to earth, including its orbit.

The molecule does not go before St. Paul, St. Peter or God to stand judgment and await the decision of god -whether you have to go to heaven or hell- because there is no hell and there is no heaven the way we understand hell and heaven.

So it does not matter whether you are a Muslim, a Christian, a Jew, a Buddhist or a believer in any other religion.

The molecule (Bubble) enters the original blueprint of "YOU"; meaning the first copy, the first sketch, the first formula that created you. Humans came from a blueprint. Every human being has a double. Your double is a copy stored in the "Rouh-Plasma"; a compartment under the control of the Anunnaki on Nibiru and can be transported to another star, if Nibiru ceases to exist. And this double is immortal.

In this context, human is immortal, because its double never dies. Once the molecule re-enters your original copy (Which is the original You), you come back to life with all your faculties, including your memory, but without physical, emotional and sensorial properties (The properties you had on earth), because they are not perfect."

Ulema Sadik said: "At that time, and only at that time, you will decide whether to stay in your double or go somewhere else...the universe is yours. If your past life on earth accumulated enough good deeds such as charity, generosity, compassion, forgiveness, goodness, mercy, love for animals, respect for nature, gratitude, fairness, honesty, loyalty...then your double will have all the wonderful opportunities and reasons to decide and select what shape, format, condition you will be in, and where you will continue to live."

In other words, you will have everything, absolutely everything and you can have any shape you want including a brand new corporal form. You will be able to visit the whole universe and live for ever, as a mind, as an indestructible presence, and also as a non-physical, non- earthly body, but you can still re-manifest yourself in any physical body you wish to choose.

Worth mentioning here, that the molecule, (So-called soul in terrestrial term) enters a mew dimension by shooting itself into space and passing through the "Bab", a sort of a celestial star-gate or entrance.

If misguided, your molecule (So-called your soul) will be lost for ever in the infinity of time and space and what there is between., until reconnected to your prototype via the "Miraya".

Is the afterlife a physical world?

According to the Anunnaki Ulema: "No and yes. Because life after death unites time and space and everything that it constitutes space and time.

It means extending to, and encompassing everything in the universe, and everything you saw, knew, felt, liked and disliked. Everything you have experienced on earth exists in other dimensions, and there are lots of them. Everything you saw on earth has its duplicate in another dimension.

Even your past, present and future on earth have another past, another present and another future in other worlds and other dimensions.

And if you are lucky and alert, you can create more pasts, more presents and more futures, and continue to live in new wonderful worlds and dimensions; this happens after you die. Anunnaki and some of their messengers and remnants on earth can do that.

The physical aspect of the afterlife can be recreated the way you want it by using your Fik'r. Yes, you can return to earth as a visitor, and see all the shows and musicals on Broadway or hang out on Les Champs-Elysées.

You can also talk to many people who died if you can find their double in the afterlife.

You can also enjoy the presence of your pets (Dead or alive), and continue to read a book you didn't finish while still alive on earth. What you currently see on earth is a replica of what there is beyond earth and beyond death.

The afterlife is also non physical, because it has different properties, density and ways of life."

Anunnaki Ulema W Lin said: "Through Fik'r, a person can enter higher dimensions. It is of a major importance to train your Fik'r. "Transmission of the mind" training sessions can develop extra-sensorial faculties and open your "inner eye" commonly referred to as the Third Eye..."

*** *** ***

121

Metaphysical-religious context:
"Although the Anunnaki do not believe in the same god we worship, revere and fear, understanding their concept of Khalek, the creator of our universe (Our galaxy), other galaxies, the whole universe and especially life after death (The afterlife) could change the way we understand "God", the universe, the reason for our existence on earth, the principle of immortality, because it opens up a new way to comprehend the place of Man in the universe in this life and all the ones beyond the frontiers of time and space...", said Ulema Ghandar.

"The Anunnaki-Ulema's view of the afterlife gives a great hope and an immense relief to human beings...to all of us...", added Ulema Stambouli.
According to the "Book of Rama-Dosh", the only Anunnaki's manuscript left on earth in the custody of the Ul'ma (Ulema), humans should not be afraid to die, nor fear what is going to happen to them after they die. SinharMarduck, an Anunnaki leader and scholar said human life continues after death in the form of "Intelligence" stronger than any form of energy known to mankind.
And because it is mental, the deceased human will never suffer again; there are no more pain, financial worries, punishment, hunger, violence or any of the anxiety, stress, poverty and serious daily concerns that create confusion and unhappiness for the human beings.

After death, the human body never leaves earth, nor comes back to life by an act of god, Jesus, or any Biblical prophet. This body is from dirt, and to dirt it shall return. That's the end of the story.
Inside our body, there is not what we call "Soul".
Soul is an invention of mankind. It does not exist anywhere inside us.
Instead, there is a non-physical substance called Fik'r that makes the brain function, and it is the brain that keeps the body working, not the soul.
The Fik'r was created by the Anunnaki at the time they created us.

122

The Fik'r, although it is the primordial source of life for our physical body, it is not to be considered as DNA, because DNA is a part of Fik'r; DNA is the physical description of our genes, a sort of a series of formulas, numbers and sequences of what there is in our body, the data and history of our genes, genetic origin, ethnicity, race, so on.
The Fik'r contains the DNA and all its genetic data.

*** *** ***

VII. Fikrama "Fikr-Rama":
Name of the human brain's sixth wave, unknown yet to science.
It is related to An-zalubirach, also known as Tarkiz; a mental training that develops a supernatural power.
To fully understand what Kikrama "Fikr-Rama" means, we must first comprehend what An-zalubirach is, and how it works.

An-zalubirach is an Ana'kh/Ulemite term meaning the following:
- **a-**Collecting thoughts, receiving and sending multiple mental images via brain wave synchronization, to improve mental and physical health;
- **b-**Using mental energy to move or teleport things.

This is one of the phases and practices of Tarkiz.
Tarkiz means deep mental or intellectual concentration that produces telekinesis and teleportation phenomena. Ulema's students learn this technique in various forms.
Basically it works like this:
- **a-**The students use their Conduit (Which is located in the brain's cells) to control the waves of their brains (First level of learning).
- **b-**The students concentrate on an object hidden behind a screen or a divider made from thin rice paper. (Second level of learning)
By synchronizing the frequency of their Conduit and an absolute state of introspection, the students attempt to move the hidden object from one place to another without even touching it.

123

In a more advanced stage, the students attempt to alter the properties of the object by lowering or increasing the frequencies and vibrations of the object itself.

The brain is constantly producing different types of frequencies, waves, and vibrations, and transmitting various messages based on our mental activity, feelings, thoughts, and state of consciousness or mind.

Thus, the brain waves are divided in four states or categories called:

1-Beta
2-Alpha
3-Theta
4-Delta

In addition to Betha, Alpha, Theta, and Delta, the Anunnaki Ulema developed a sixth wave called Fikr-Rama. It is neither measurable nor detectable, because it does not emanate from the physical brain.

It is triggered by the Conduit situated in the brain's cells. No science on earth can direct us to the exact position of the Conduit.

Let me explain this process:

- **1-**Through the mechanism of the Conduit, the enlightened ones regulate mind's waves and frequencies.
- **2-**The Fikr-Rama allows them to enter other dimensions, solid substances and matter.
- **3-**The Fikr-Rama is a sort of a beam much lighter than laser. It does not have particles.
- **4-**It has no substance per se, yet, it contains energy.
- **5-**Extraterrestrials in general, and Anunnaki in particular have a multitude of similar brain's waves.
- **6-**The Fikr-Rama is one single tone in the rainbow of their mental vibrations.
- **7-**Highly advanced extraterrestrial beings can project thoughts and holographic images using any of their mental vibrations waves.

VIII. Kira-Fik:
Composed from two words:
- **a**-Kira (From Kira'at) means reading,
- **b**-Fik (From Fk'r) meaning mind.

The general meaning is the development, or the activation of telepathy in the brain of an Anunnaki student. Before the pre-final phase of an Anunnaki student purification, what happens takes only one minute, and this is the most important procedure done for each Anunnaki student on the first day of his/her studies – the creation of the mental "Conduit."

A new identity is created for each Anunnaki student by the development of a new pathway in his or her mind, connecting the student to the rest of the Anunnaki's psyche. Simultaneously, the cells check with the "other copy" of the mind and body of the Anunnaki student, to make sure that the "Double" and "Other Copy" of the Mind and body of the student are totally clean. During this phase, the Anunnaki student temporarily loses his or her memory, for a very short time.

This is how the telepathic faculty is developed, or enhanced in everyone.

It is necessary, since to serve the total community of the Anunnaki, the individual program inside each Anunnaki student is immediately shared with everybody. Incidentally, this is why there is such a big difference between extra-terrestrial and human telepathy.

On earth, no one ever succeeds in emptying the whole metal content from human cells like the Anunnaki are so adept in doing, and the Conduit cannot be formed.

Lacking the Conduit that is built for each Anunnaki, the human mind is not capable in communication with the extra-terrestrials.

However, don't think for a moment that there is any kind of invasion of privacy.

The simplistic idea of any of your friends tapping into your private thoughts does not exist for the Anunnaki.

Their telepathy is rather complicated. The Anunnaki have collective intelligence and individual intelligence. And this is directly connected to two things:

- **a**-The first is the access to the "Community Depot of Knowledge" that any Anunnaki can tap in and update and acquire additional knowledge.
- **b**-The second is an "Individual Prevention Shield," also referred to as "Personal Privacy."

This means that an Anunnaki can switch on and off hir/her direct link (a channel) to other Anunnaki. By establishing the "Screen" or "Filter" an Anunnaki can block others from either communicating with him or her, or simply preventing others from reading his or her personal thoughts.

"Filter", "Screen" and "Shield" are interchangeably used to describe the privacy protection. In addition, an Anunnaki can program telepathy and set it up on chosen channels, exactly as we turn on our radio set and select the station we wish to listen to. Telepathy has several frequency, channels and stations.

*** *** ***

CHAPTER 8
The Mind, the Brain and Supersymetric Mind

- Afik-r'-Tanawar.
- Alal-ra.
- Brain "The Supersymetric Mind".
- 1. Introduction.
- 2. Excerpts from Ulema Sorenztein's Kira'at.
- 3. The Supersymetric Mind.
- a. A brief note on supersymetry.
- b. What is a "Supersymetric Mind"?
- Levels of the Mind "lama".
- 1. Definition and introduction.
- 2. "All humans have more than one brain".

*** *** ***

CHAPTER 8
The Mind, the Brain and Supersymetric Mind

Afik-r'-Tanawar:
Enlightenment through the development of the mind. Composed of two words;
*   **a**-Afik-r, which means mind.
*   **b**-Tanawar, which means the act of illumination.

The Anunnaki have created us on earth to serve their needs.
Their intentions were to create a race that could carry heavy physical load and do intense physical labor.
This was the initial and prime objective. Thus, the "Naphsiya" (DNA) they put in us had limited lifespan, and mental faculties.
Later on, they discovered that they had to prolong the human lifespan and add more developed mental faculties, so they added the Hara-Kiya (Internal energy or physical strength).

Few generations later, the early human beings stock evolves considerably, because the Anunnaki added fully operational Mind in the human body.
To do so, they installed a Conduit with limited capabilities. In the same time, this Conduit was also installed into the prototype of the human body.
Thus, through the Mind, the physical body of the humans got linked to the Double.

This non-physical link created a Fourth dimension for all of us.
In fact, it did not create a Fourth dimension per se, rather it activated it.
So now, at that stage, humans had a physical dimension (Life on earth), and not-a-totally separated non-physical dimension called Nafis-Ra.
So, the Bashar (Humans) became destined to acquire two dimensions, as exactly the Anunnaki decided.

129

Later on, centuries upon centuries, the human mind began to evolve, because the other Mind, call it now the Double or prototype began to evolve simultaneously and in sync.

The more the prototype is advanced the more the "Physical Mind" becomes alert, creative and multidimensional. But we are not trapped, and our mind is no longer conditioned by the Anunnaki.

The Anunnaki gave us all the choices, opportunities, freewill and freedom to learn on our own and progress. This is why we are accountable and responsible for everything we do and think about.

Because of the evolution of our mind, and realization of an inner knowledge of our surroundings, and understanding what is right and what is wrong, a major mental faculty emerged in all of us: Conscience."

*** *** ***

Alal-ra:
A mental channel implanted in the brain by the Anunnaki's geneticists to send and receive information telepathically.

*** *** ***

Brain "The Supersymetric Mind"
Study of the influence of the Anunnaki's programming of our brain and fate.

- 1. Introduction
- 2. Excerpts from Ulema Sorenztein's Kira'at
- 3. The Supersymetric Mind
- a. A brief note on supersymetry
- b. What is a "Supersymetric Mind"?

1. Introduction:
Honorable Ulema Sorenstein once said, "...in many cases, some people are responsible for their own bad luck and failure in life. It all depends on what you put in your Araya/Conduit brain zones."

He added: "Even though, the human mind was created the way the Anunnaki wanted it, and even though, your brain had been programmed and fashioned 65,000 years ago, and "upgraded" and reconditioned by the Anunnaki some 6,000 to 7,000 years ago, you can still bring important changes to your mind, and make it work for you like a charm."

He continued:
"Everything depends on:

- 1-How to store your ideas and thoughts in your brain;
- 2-Which idea, thought, or vision will you consciously allow to enter your brain;
- 3-How to control the vibrations of your ideas, visions, and thoughts;
- 4-How to scan your ideas, visions, and thoughts that are stored on the Araya net;
- 5-How to stabilize the vibrations of your mind;
- 6-How to get rid of bad thoughts and symptoms of a "weak personality" that prevent you from succeeding in life and getting a good job;
- 7-How to prevent the vibrations of a bad thought from deteriorating or "killing" the vibrations of good thoughts, etc...
- And something else you should remember, you are not the slave of the genetic creation of the Anunnaki who created all of us."

*** *** ***

131

Note:

Ulema Sorenstein is a modern American Ulema, originally from
Latvia. He lived in Lower Manhattan area in New York City, and
he is 135 year old. You look at him, and you don't give him more
than 37. Many people have seen him in different places,
simultaneously. I will comment later on what he meant by:
a-"Responsible for their own bad luck and failure",
b- "Araya/Conduit";
c- "Brain zones".
But first, let's listen to his Anunnaki-Ulema Kira'at on success
and failure in life, and in business.

*** *** ***

2. Excerpts from Ulema Sorenstein's Kira'at
(As is, and unedited):

- Many of you came to me and asked me why some people
  are luckier than others?
- Or why Elizabeth is making more money than Patricia?
- Or why this person is more successful than another
  person, knowing well that he is a spiritual and a good
  man, and also very intelligent, while the other person is
  less spiritual and not so bright?
- Does intelligence or morality has anything to do with
  success in life, and/or the way our brain was wired by
  the Anunnaki, at the time they created us?
- My answer to you is this: Intelligence is very important
  but does not always guarantee success in life. Many great
  inventors died penniless.
- Morality is very important in life, but many spiritual
  people were murdered because of their moral principles.
- Morality and intelligence have nothing to do with your
  success in life (Your life on this Earth.)

- The high standard of morality and intelligence of a person does not change luck, decrease or increase your luck and success in your life.
- I guess, you are concerned with social success, financial success, or something like that. Well, let's talk about your financial success and success in your career.
- I will take an example from your modern city, from your modern life, from your modern society where you live, so you will understand me perfectly.
- In 1989, Melissa, Peggy, and Esther graduated from NYU with a doctorate degree in education.
- They have identical credentials, and three of them are of the same age.
- They are healthy, and intelligent, and want to succeed in life.
- Usually, when you are not an entrepreneur, you look for a job. Melissa, Peggy, and Esther are not entrepreneurs. Their greatest asset is their academic advanced degree. Very good.
- In the modern world of science, education, technology, and knowledge, education is extremely important, and a degree should help a lot.
- A few years later, let's say 1999 for example, you learned that Melissa became the Secretary of Education; Peggy is a high school teacher in San Diego; and Esther is working as a telemarketer in Brooklyn.
- Now, we start to wonder, how come Melissa got a very prestigious and a high profile job in Washington, while Peggy and Esther did not?
- After all, if credentials are required, all of them have the same qualifications and same credentials. So what is going on here?
- Why Peggy is working as a school teacher, and not as a superintendent or director of the school in San Diego, or as an education commissioner?
- And why Esther is working as a telemarketer getting $10 or $15 an hour?

133

- What did happen to these three highly educated and lovely ladies?
- Image makers, public relations advisors, headhunters, human resources directors, and even psychologists will avalanche you with all sorts of reasons, ranging from personality, contact, luck, political or social affiliations, ambition, job search strategies, networking, location, and even because the way a resume was written.
- All these reasons and explanations have some merits. But they do not explain why Esther could not get a better job, or at least a better pay, taking into consideration the doctorate degree she has earned. After all, such a high academic degree requires a sound and developed mind, knowledge, determination, perseverance, and analytical approach to things in life. All these qualities should have served and helped Esther in finding a better job.
- Well, the Ulema have a different explanation.
- Although, the Ulema recognize the validity, practicality, and importance of the explanations given by those experts in the field, the Ulema believe that what you call "Luck", success and prosperity are already fashioned, and written on the front page of the book of your life.
- What was already decided upon vis-à-vis your success in life can be found (And sometime changed and totally transformed by your own will) in the Araya Zones of your brain. A brain that was genetically created by the Anunnaki. And I am going to explain to you what I mean by Araya, brain's zone, Conduit's activation, and your genetic brain.
- Now, you have to remember that everything in the world emits vibrations.
- And all sorts of vibrations occupy a place in the world.
- Some vibrations are detectable, some are not.
- Some vibrations, modern science recognizes, detects, and registers, and some are not yet known to science and mental health empiric efforts.
- The same thing is happening right now in your brain.

134

- The word "world" means everything that surrounds you, including distant planets, galaxies and extra-dimensions.
- The "world" also means the infinitesimal zones in the Araya which is in your brain.
- The Araya is the domain, the realm, the landscape where 73 different zones of your brain are found.
- Each zone of the Araya functions differently, because it was created, engineered and programmed differently by the Anunnaki, at the time the prototypes and final "models" of the human race were created.
- And yes, the $10 per hour Esther is getting as a telemarketer in Brooklyn has a lot to do with the Araya, and one region of her Araya.
- I am getting there. Be very patient with me. If you are not patient and you rush to a speedy answer, you will miss the boat, and you will become very confused.
- At the end of the Kira'at, everything will become clear to you.
- Now, let's go back to the vibrations. Every thought, each idea you have in your brain, has a vibration. And each vibration occupies a spot in your Araya, called "Jaba".
- Let's simply things and call Araya now a net.
- This net has many holes, called "Jabas".
- Each Jaba (A hole, so to speak) stores one idea.
- And each idea or thought in the Jaba of the net produces a vibration.
- For example, if the net has 70,000 Jabas, your brain will be able to store 70,000 ideas and thoughts.
- This means, that your Araya hosts 70,000 vibrations. And that is full capacity.
- Some people who are more creative than you could have 300,000 ideas and thoughts stored in 300,000 Jabas (Holes or locations) in your Araya (Net).
- The good thoughts and good ideas in your Araya do not expand. They stay well balanced and well synchronized where they are (Inside the Jaba of the net).

135

- There, they are safe and protected.
- Only bad thoughts, and bad ideas, such as fear, low self-esteem, stubbornness, hate, indecisiveness, laziness, tendency toward violence, badmouthing people, envy, jealousy, betrayal, so on, emit vibrations that overflow the perimeter (Circumference) of the Jaba (Hole or location) that stores your thought or idea.
- This phenomenon (Overflow) takes over the adjacent Jaba(s) containing a good idea or a good thought.
- Because the negative energy inside your mind is usually stronger than the positive energy of a good thought, the Jaba on the net (Location) containing a good thought or a good idea shrinks, gets contaminated, and stops to emit positive and creative energy.
- This, kills the good thoughts and good ideas in your Araya.
- If this continues, all good and creative ideas and thoughts in your brain will be damaged and neutralized by your bad thoughts and ideas.
- This will stop your creativity.
- In other words, many cells in your brain's or Araya's, and their creative mental faculties stored in the Jaba become dysfunctional; atrophied or dead.
- In this case, you are responsible for causing this deterioration. Nobody has forced you to think about bad thoughts or bad ideas. It is your own doing.
- You might say, I have no control over all this.
- Things happen. Ideas come and go.
- And I will tell you, you are wrong, because you can control your ideas and your thoughts, and make them work for you in a very healthy, positive and productive way.
- I will explain to you how you can do that very shortly.
- The most destructive thoughts that prevent you from succeeding in life are:
- a-Low self-esteem;

- b-Fear (Fear of anything);
- c-Unwillingness to accept new ideas;
- d-Bitterness;
- e-Constantly contradicting others because you have developed a complex of inferiority, and not because of a complex of superiority;
- f-Negativity.

Note: a to f are not categorically part of the Anunnaki's primordial (Original) makeup of the genetic creation of your mind. Your upbringing, way or life, and personal vision of the world and your immediate environment could have caused this.

- Let's go back to Esther' situation, and see whether the Anunnaki are responsible for a lack of a great success in her life, considering the very advanced academic degree she earned, or whether Esther's own actions, thoughts, personality, or her bad "luck" prevented her from getting a better job.
- And above all, let's see what the Ulema recommend.
- In life, we have to simplify things to understand them. So, let's approach Esther's situation in a very simple manner.
- It is more likely that a, b, d, and f, have created the unpleasant condition of Esther.
- The symptoms a, b, d, and f, emanate negative and destructive vibrations in the Araya, causing the Jaba(s) to shrink.
- And when the Jaba(s) shrink, the human being ceased to become creative and resourceful.
- The vibrations of a, b, d, and f overflow the Jaba. And you already know what happens when the overflow occurs and invades other Jabas.

137

- The lack of creative thinking and resourcefulness blended with negativity and low self-esteem will prevent any person from getting the kind of job or occupation, she/he deserved.
- And this is exactly what happened to Esther.
- In the Jaba(s), the Anunnaki have installed and implanted sequences of ideas, thoughts and faculties that shape the future and the "human cosmography" of all humans.
- The symptoms a, b, d, and f, were never the primordial ingredients of the Araya or the Jaba.
- This is very good, because it shows that the human race is not enslaved by the genetic makeup/design of the human race, by the Anunnaki.
- Many writers, and conspiracy theories advocates in the Western hemisphere, and particularly in the United States, so erroneously have claimed that the Anunnaki are controlling the world.
- The Anunnaki are our masters; the human race is enslaved by the Anunnaki; the governments of the world are controlled by the Anunnaki.
- This is untrue.
- But what is true is that the brain as designed by the Anunnaki cannot escape or go beyond the genetic specifications of the Anunnaki.
- However, the Anunnaki have no absolute control over our brain, (Araya, and Jabas), since they have allowed us to activate the "Conduit" in our brain.
- And since all of us have more than one "single brain", wonderful things can be accomplished, and our freedom will always be protected.
- The Ulema believe that the human brain is in fact a "Supersymetric Brain".
- And I will explain this to you.

138

- Because once you fully understand how your "Supersymetric Brain" functions, you will be able to make miracles, and heal yourself from many things.
- But you should never ever claim, that the Anunnaki-Ulema's healing and therapy methods do replace or substitute for any traditional, and scientific means and methods of treatment, and diagnosis, as applied in traditional medicine, and/or in other legitimate mental health practices.

*** *** ***

3. "Ma bira-rach" the "Supersymetric Mind":

Excerpts from Ulema Sorenstein's Kira'at, as is, and unedited:

a. A brief note on supersymetry:

According to the theory of supersymetry, also known as SUSY, all particles in the known universe have their counter-part, also called super-partner(s).

Basically, this is the view of quantum physics scientists and theorists. In the Anunnaki-Ulema context, supersymetry is either the similar or the opposite of YOU.

In a limited sense, it is the other super-partner of "you", and what constitutes you at all levels; organically, bio-organically, chemically, genetically, etherically, atomically, mentally and physically.

The most important and predominant part of your mind-body supersymetry is your mind.

Because everything starts in your mind.

In this context, your mind is a "Supersymetric Mind".

*** *** ***

139

b. What is a "Supersymetric Mind"?

- You were brought up to believe that every person in the world has a brain; one single brain.
- Nobody seems to contradict this. And I do not contradict this either.
- However, this "single brain" is not the only brain you have, at least in this dimension.
- All of us, enlightened or not have two brains; the first brain is the one we are aware of, and familiar with, from studying anatomy, medicine and other disciplines, and the other mind, is the one that co-existed, and currently co-exists side-by-side your brain, and outside your body.
- It is called the supersymetric mind. In Ana'kh, it is called "Ma bira-rach".
- For now, let's compare Ma bira-rach to your "Double".
- As you already know, the Double means the etheric image of your physical body.
- Ma bira-rach is the etheric image of your brains.
- But we call it supersymetric, because the particles constituting the physical and etheric mind can de detected and scanned scientifically.
- In the Western hemisphere, and particularly in the United States, the theory of supersymetry has received a warm welcome in the scientific community.
- Scanning the physical brain has become a scientific reality. But scanning the etheric brain has never been done in the West.
- The Anunnaki-Ulema (Mounawariin) know how to scan both the physical and etheric substance of your brains. And I have to remind you here, that you should never ever attempt to scan your mind or others' mind using any means or methods that constitute and illegal medical practice. Leave it to physicians, medical technicians, and those who are authorized by the law to do so.
- Two methods have been used by the Anunnaki-Ulema to scan the brains (Mind).

- One is purely scientific; the other is metascientific, which is totally incomprehensible and unrealistic to Western scientists.
- The Anunnaki-Ulema's scientific method consists of implanting on the "surface of the tissues" of your brains mobile microscopic devices that move around and scan the Jaba(s) of you brains.
- The devices detect tumors, deterioration of the cells, and repair the damaged cells.
- In the United States, some have compared these devices to the very small metallic objects, an extraterrestrial race (Greys) has implanted inside the bodies of abductees. This is totally incorrect.
- According to some legitimate physicians (involved with some sort of ufology in the United States,) who have treated those abductees, these devices are of an "alien substance and origin".
- The main function of these alien devices is to monitor the abductees, and to serve as "receiver-emitter" of aliens' messages.
- I will not comment on their claims.
- But one thing I will tell you for sure: The Anunnaki-Ulema implants are not tracking devices.
- Because once, the cell damages are repaired, the implants disintegrate, lose their mass, and the human body flushed them out, the normal way.
- The Anunnaki-Ulema scientific mind (Brains) scanning occurs in that manner.
- The scanning is a physical and a real operation.
- This idea might seem strange and absurd to many scientists in the West.
- However, we have learned that many military scientists, psychiatrists, and surgeons, in the West are exploring these techniques.
- My prediction is that in the very near future, the United States of America will be using these devices implants techniques in hospitals and medical facilities.

141

- As to the second Anunnaki-Ulema etheric mind scanning techniques, well, these techniques are taught to our students, and do not require a surgical operation.
- You can scan the mind, and bring comfort to your mind and your body by either activating the Conduit or superposing the Araya (Net of the mind) of your physical mind and the Araya of your supersymetric mind (Your other mind that exists as a bulk of separate particles in an etheric substance.)
- Using this second technique, you will be able to neutralize the vibrations of the cells storing bad thoughts and bad ideas, such as bitterness, negativity, lack of energy, laziness, indecisiveness, and fear.
- This second technique is called "Ma bi-idawa".
- I will explain Ma bi idawa in my next Kira'at.

*** *** ***

Notes:
1-Ma bi idawa is outlined and explained in the book "The Revised, Indexed and Complete Book of the Anunnaki Ulema Final Warning: Humanity destiny, UFOs threat, and the extraterrestrials final solution", and in the book "Anunnaki Self Healing."

2-The Anunnaki-Ulema scientific mind (Brains) scanning via devices implants in the human body is not science fiction literature.

Allegedly, surgeons and psychiatrists who worked on the CIA Mind Control Program in the fifties, sixties, and early seventies have attempted to develop and implement quasi-similar techniques on volunteers, and retarded patients.

3-Most recently, a vast literature and avalanches of scientific papers on this subject appear in the American scientific community, and many physicians, scientists, and futurists advanced mind-boggling theories on these implants techniques, on a theoretical level.

142

Nevertheless, what was theory in the past is nowadays a pragmatic application and standard procedures in many scientific fields.

*** *** ***

Levels of the Mind "Iama":
1. Definition and introduction
2. "All humans have more than one brain"

1. Definition and introduction:
A term referring to the concept of the different "Levels of the Mind". According to many authors and thinkers, the human brain is a depot of all knowledge we have acquired so far.
This is not totally correct, according to the Book of Ramadosh.

Ulema Oppenheimer said verbatim, as is and unedited: "The physical brain, or in other words, the brain of a human being living here on Earth is one of the multiple layers of an infinite series of knowledge and experience acquired by a person in and outside the barrier of time and space.
Meaning that every single human being, regardless of the level of his or her intelligence and social status has an infinite number of other brains "Minds" fully operational in different and multiple spheres, times and spaces.
And this includes the landscape of our Solar System, and other universes' systems. This is the cause and effect of the creation of the Universe and Man.

*** *** ***

2. "All humans have more than one brain":
Man cannot be separated from the universe, because he is a vital and primordial part of its molecules.

143

In other words, a person can be very intelligent and extremely important in this life, and in the same time, he can be a total ignorant and unimportant in other life that co-exists simultaneously somewhere else in the universe."

He added "here on Earth you might be an amateur musician, and in other world you are a conductor of symphonic orchestra, or even equal to Mozart.

In each dimension, and this includes stars and planets, you as a human being you live a separate life, and you have a totally independent brain. Some Enlightened Masters are fully capable of synchronizing both, and even more..."

*** *** ***

Chapter 9
The Anunnaki Ulema Teachings on Immortality

- Does everybody reach immortality?
- Have the Anunnaki made us immortal?
- Question: Do we become immortal if we follow the teachings of the Ulema?
- Answer of the honorable Ulema:
- Can hybrids reach immortality?
- Did the Anunnaki kings on earth seek immortality?
- Gilgamesh's visits to Baalbeck and Al Arz
- What did the Anunnaki's leaders tell the Ulema about our humans' longevity on earth and immortality in the other world?
- Can we live for ever?
- Question: A student asked the Ulema this question: Can we live for ever with the angels in heaven? Are human immortal since we are the creation of God who is immortal himself?
- You can live 10,000 years on earth, if you comply with the rules of the Ulema's Nizam
- The most important requirements/prerequisites (Moutawajibaat, Shou-Rout) to acquire longevity or immortality are
- The most important rules (Kawa-ed, Ousool) to acquire longevity or immortality are

*** *** ***

Chapter 9
The Anunnaki Ulema Teachings on Immortality

The following is taken from a Kira'a by an Ulema, dialogues with students, and an honorable teacher's answers to questions by novices.

***   ***   ***

Does everybody reach immortality? Have the Anunnaki made us immortal?

The following is taken from a Kira'a by an Ulema, dialogues with students, and an honorable teacher's answers to questions by novices.

Question: Do we become immortal if we follow the teachings of the Ulema?

Answer of the honorable Ulema:

- On earth, humans cannot reach immortality. Afterlife, the "Tahirin" (Purified ones) will reach immortality.
- But we have to understand what immortality is? Is it an eternal existence? What kind of existence? Is it physical or spiritual? Mental or organic? Terrestrial or extraterrestrial? Nothing in the universe lasts for ever, not even the universe itself. Eventually, the universe will cease to exist once it has reached the limitations of its expansion.

Note: Contemporary leading scientists in the field of cosmology and quantum physics agree with the honorable Ulema.

147

They have publicly stated, that soon or later, the universe will cease to exist. Those who believe in Jesus, Mohammad, Krishna, Vishnu, Jehovah, and Allah don't.)

- It is very important to keep in mind, that so many extraterrestrial beings came to earth, thousands of years ago. We are aware of 46 different alien races who have visited planet earth.
- Some of these alien races created early forms of human beings. I say forms, because at the time these living creatures were created by the aliens, they lacked mental faculties. Some looked like us, but not exactly.
- We know from the manuscripts of Melkart and the "Society of the Fish" which was established by the early Phoenicians who lived on the Island of Arwad, that the primitive human beings were called "Intelligent animals" because they behaved and lived like animals, but were more intelligent than the beasts of the earth.
- These beings were created by extraterrestrials who came from a lower dimension, even though, they were highly advanced.
- The extraterrestrials did not install a Conduit in the brain cells of the primitive beings.
- Without a Conduit, no living creature can ascend to the Madkhal or Ba'ab. Consequently, a passage to the Fourth dimension is virtually impossible without a Conduit.
- Thus, these primitive creatures did not reach immortality, because they did not go through the Ba'ab.
- Because they did not have a mind, but brain's membranes, they were unable to continue to live afterlife.
- In the afterlife, you continue to live only with your mind.
- Your mind is the source of energy that keeps you alive.
- The primitive creatures did not have a mind, although their brain was wired like an electronic machine.
- Their brain was not developed at all, and as a result, their race became extinct.

- They perished, not because of famine, wars, or fall of asteroids on earth, but because of the deterioration of the cells of their brains.
- You will not find these primitive creatures on other planets, or in parallel dimensions.
- Humans who were "Dha-kiliyan" (Genetically) created by the Anunnaki will eventually reach immortality, as long as the universe remains in existence.
- The early living-forms of humans, primitive creatures, intelligent animals, monstrous robotic human-like species vanished from the face of the earth some 65,000-61,000 years ago.
- When the Igigi came to planet earth, some 65,000 years ago, they captured many of those primitive half human, half animal creatures who were living in Australia, Madagascar, Brazil, Indonesia, Central Africa and some regions of Europe, and transformed them Dha-kiliyan (Genetically) into an upgraded form of humans. Still, they looked like robotic animals. A few years later, they died out.
- Some 65,000-60,000 years ago, three extraterrestrial races Dha-kiliyan (Genetically) created a new human race. They were the Lyrans, the Nordics, and the Anunnaki. The newly created human race had a mind (Not to be confused with soul), brains' cells and a dormant Conduit.
- Because a Conduit was installed in their brains, our ancestors were destined to reach immortality. Today, we are the offspring and descendants of the intelligent human race created by these three extraterrestrial races.
- Yes, you can say, the Anunnaki made us immortals.

*** *** ***

149

Can hybrids reach immortality?

The following is taken from a Kira'a by an Ulema, dialogues with students, and an honorable teacher's answers to questions by novices.

Answer of the honorable Ulema:

- Although hybrids are intelligent beings, they are not to be considered neither as humans nor as extraterrestrials.
- Their essence (DNA) is not pure.
- They are genetically created either by humans or by a malicious extraterrestrial race.
- Any living creature Dha-kiliyan (Genetically) created by humans will never reach immortality.
- Because a Dha-kiliyi (Genetic) creation of other living-forms manufactured by human beings is an artificial product, this Dha-kiliyi (Genetic) product which does not include the first energy element introduced in regular human beings by the Anunnaki will totally disintegrate without leaving the "Shou'la" (Spark of life).
- The Shou' la was created on earth by the Anunnaki. No human ever succeeded in duplicating a Shou'la.
- Any living creature Dha-kiliyan (Genetically) created on earth or in other physical dimensions by a malicious extraterrestrial race coming from a lower dimension will not reach immortality. (Author's note: I do believe that the honorable Ulema was referring to what American ufologists call the "Greys", even though, he has never used the word "Greys".
- It is my belief that this word is an American ufology terminology. The word he used was "Min Kariji al-dounia". Min means from. Kariji means outside or outer. Dounia means the world.

150

- Living entities and hybrids created by the Greys are born contaminated.
- The Greys' contamination prevents these living entities (Hybrids, half humans-half-extraterrestrials) from ascending to the Ba'ab.
- Consequently, the hybrids will not enter the other dimensions and reach immortality.

*** *** ***

What did the Anunnaki's leaders tell the Ulema about our humans' longevity on earth and immortality in the other world?

Can we live for ever?
Masters of esoterism believe that man could live for ever, whether in this dimension or in the other. Because the teachings of the Ulema are not based on esoterism, but rather on the Anunnaki's metaphysics and science, the immortality of Man is no longer a speculative matter for the Ulema and their initiated students.
However, many of the Ulema's students (Almost 99% of novices were initiated, and eventually became enlightened) in their initial training stage were perplexed by the idea, and during the early stage of their training asked so many questions about Man's longevity, immortality and the after-life.

*** *** ***

The following is taken from a Kira'a by an Ulema, dialogues with students, and an honorable teacher's answers to questions by novices.

Question:
A student asked the Ulema this question: Can we live for ever with the angels in heaven?
Are human immortal since we are the creation of God who is immortal himself?

151

Note: It is obvious that that question was asked by a student who has not yet received advanced training or attended readings of a high level, because he used words and sentences such as "creation of God" and "angels in heaven".

The Anunnaki and the Ulema do not believe in the same God we worship and fear; the Judeo-Christian-Muslim God, that is, because they know the origin, nature and name of the person, entity or supreme being who introduced himself as God to Abraham, and the early Jewish prophets.

Al Mutawalli said: "That god was a fake god. He was simply one of the early royal leaders of the Anunnaki who had territorial ambitions...Some believe he was Enki, others believe he was Enlil, and eventually, one of them became Yahweh.

Abraham, and before him, his father Terah thought that the Anunnaki Sinhar was a creator, a god and ruler of heavens and earth, while in fact, he was a military Anunnaki commander in Sumer.

*** *** ***

You can live up to 10,000 years on earth, if you comply with the rules of the Ulema's Nizam

Excerpts from the answer of the honorable Ulema Rama Nabih:

- The physical cannot enter the non-physical.
- The non-physical can enter the physical and gives it life for thousands of years.
- All humans on this Earth are mortal in this sphere.
- In the future (Used as a terrestrial term), many will live thousands of years.
- The An.NA.Ki (Anunnaki) told us that some Bashar (Humans) will live for 10,000 years on planet earth. This is the maximum of their life-span in this physical dimension.

152

- Their longevity was written in their original "Shou' LA" (First sparkle of life).

Note: Today, we call it DNA.

- A modern Ulema rephrased the statement as follows: The longevity of a person is always decided upon, the moment he is born. The number of years he will live on earth is already written in his DNA.
- Man will be able to live up to 10,000 years if he complies with the Ulema's Nizam.
- The Nizam requires many things.

*** *** ***

The most important requirements/prerequisites (Moutawajibaat, Shou-Rout) to acquire longevity or immortality are:

a-Activation of the Conduit.

b-Synchronization with the Double.

c-Mental access to the Madkhal.

The most important rules (Kawa-ed, Ousool) to acquire longevity or immortality are:

a- Abstinence from eating flesh (Meaning meat).

b- Abstinence from using hallucinatory drugs.

c- Total purification of the Mind. Not even harmful thoughts and intentions are allowed. The ill-thoughts and selfish desires are as bad as ill-deeds and actions.

d- You live by thought and action. Both must remain pure and honorable.

e- Once a year, you must share one monthly earning with the poor and the needy.

f- Completion of the three levels of your training, and receiving the "Barakaat" (Blessings) of the initiation.

g- Compliance with the teachings of the Book (Book of Rama-Dosh).

The honorable teacher added:

153

- Nothing is immortal on Earth. However nothing is lost for ever on Earth. Everything is re-transformed into something else, and takes on different shapes, forms, meanings, values and dimensions...
- The longevity of Bashar (Human beings) will begin at the end of the year 2022, once the contamination of the human race has been eliminated by the Anunnaki during that year.
- In other dimensions, starting with the Fifth dimension, the Mind as you new form of existence in the universe acquires limited immortality.

*** *** ***

Books by Maximillien de Lafayette
Series: Dictionary, Lexicon, Thesaurus

SUMERIAN LANGUAGE AND CIVILIZATION
3 Volumes

De Lafayette Encyclopedic Dictionary-Lexicon of Sumerian Language And Civilization

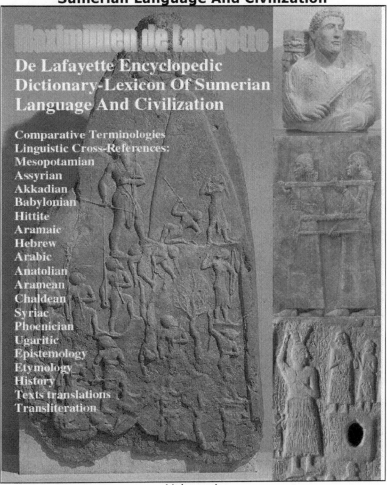

Volume I

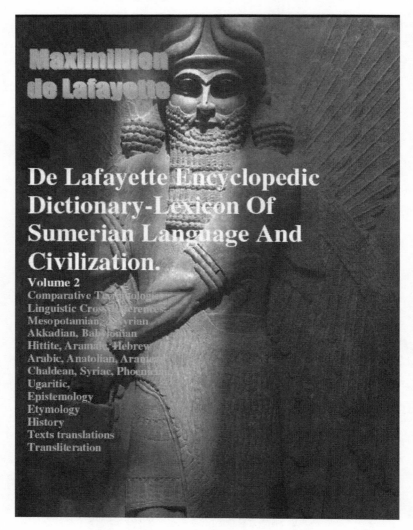

Volume II

De Lafayette Encyclopedic Dictionary-Lexicon of Sumerian Language And Civilization. Volume III

Volume III

De Lafayette Encyclopedic Thesaurus-Dictionary of Assyrian Language and Civilization. Volume I

De Lafayette Encyclopedic Thesaurus-Dictionary of Assyrian Language and Civilization

Linguistic Cross-References. Epistemology. Etymology. History. Epics' Texts translation. Transliteration. Comparative Terminologies: Aramaic. Hebrew. Chaldean. Syriac. Ugaritic. Sumerian. Akkadian. Babylonian. Hittite. Anatolian. Phoenician. Arabic and Mesopotamian

Volume I

De Lafayette Encyclopedic Thesaurus-Dictionary of Assyrian Language and Civilization. Volume II

Volume II

De Lafayette Encyclopedic Thesaurus-Dictionary of Assyrian Language and Civilization. Volume III

Volume III

De Lafayette Encyclopedic Thesaurus-Dictionary of Akkadian Language and Civilization. Volume I

Volume I

De Lafayette Encyclopedic Thesaurus-Dictionary of Akkadian Language and Civilization. Volume II

Volume II

3 Volumes
De Lafayette Encyclopedic Thesaurus-Dictionary of
Hittite Language and Civilization. Volume I.

Volume I

De Lafayette Encyclopedic Thesaurus-Dictionary of Hittite Language and Civilization. Volume II.

Volume II

De Lafayette Encyclopedic Thesaurus-Dictionary of Hittite Language and Civilization. Volume III.

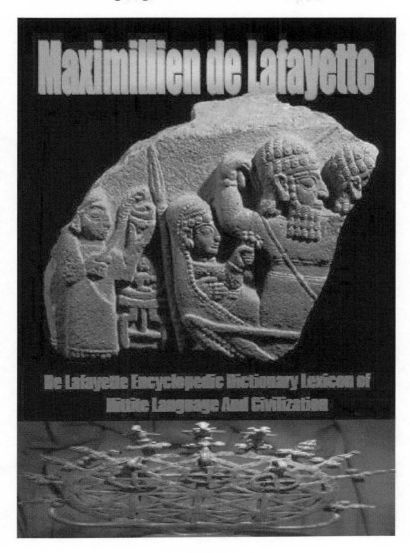

Volume III

ARAMAIC LANGUAGE AND CIVILIZATION
3 Volumes

De Lafayette Encyclopedic Dictionary of Ancient and Modern Aramaic Language and Civilization.
Volume I

De Lafayette Encyclopedic Dictionary
Of Ancient And Modern Aramaic Language And
Civilization
Comparative Lexicon Of Aramaic and Semitic Languages

Volume I

De Lafayette Encyclopedic Dictionary of Ancient and Modern Aramaic Language and Civilization.
Volume II

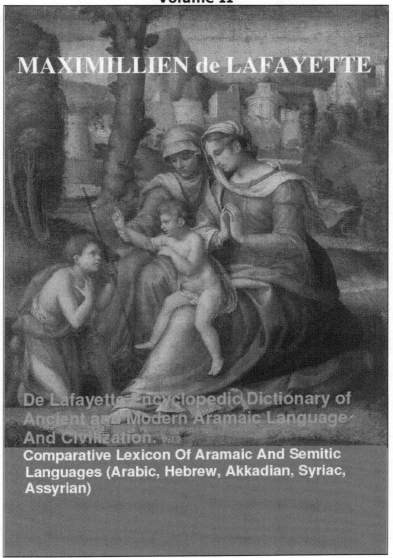

MAXIMILLIEN de LAFAYETTE

De Lafayette Encyclopedic Dictionary of Ancient and Modern Aramaic Language And Civilization. Vol.2

Comparative Lexicon Of Aramaic And Semitic Languages (Arabic, Hebrew, Akkadian, Syriac, Assyrian)

Volume II

14 ANCIENT LANGUAGE AND CIVILIZATION
14 Volumes

Thesaurus-Dictionary of Sumerian, Anunnaki, Babylonian, Mesopotamian, Assyrian, Phoenician, Aramaic, Arabic, Syriac, Anatolian, Chaldean, Hebrew, Hittite, Akkadian

Maximillien de Lafayette
Thesaurus-Dictionary of Sumerian, Anunnaki, Hittite, Babylonian, Akkadian, Assyrian, Phoenician, Aramaic. Volume 6

Including Anatolian, Mesopotamian, Chaldean, Arabic, Syriac, Hebrew
World's First Languages & Civilizations: Terminology & Relation to History, Ulema & Extraterrestrials

Maximillien de Lafayette
Anunnaki Dictionary Thesaurus
ANA'KH: LANGUAGE OF THE
EXTRATERRESTRIAL GODS AND GODDESSES

Volume I

Anunnaki Dictionary Thesaurus. Anunnaki Language and Vocabulary. Volume II

Volume II

Nibiru Manual Of Style
Guide to Anunnaki Language,
Grammar and Conversion

Volume III

NOTES

NOTES

NOTES

NOTES

Printed in the United States of America
Published by
Times Square Press. New York
A publication of
Federation of Ufology & Anunnaki Scholars, Scientists, Historians &
Authors

Visit the website of the author at:
www.maximilliendelafayettebibliography.com